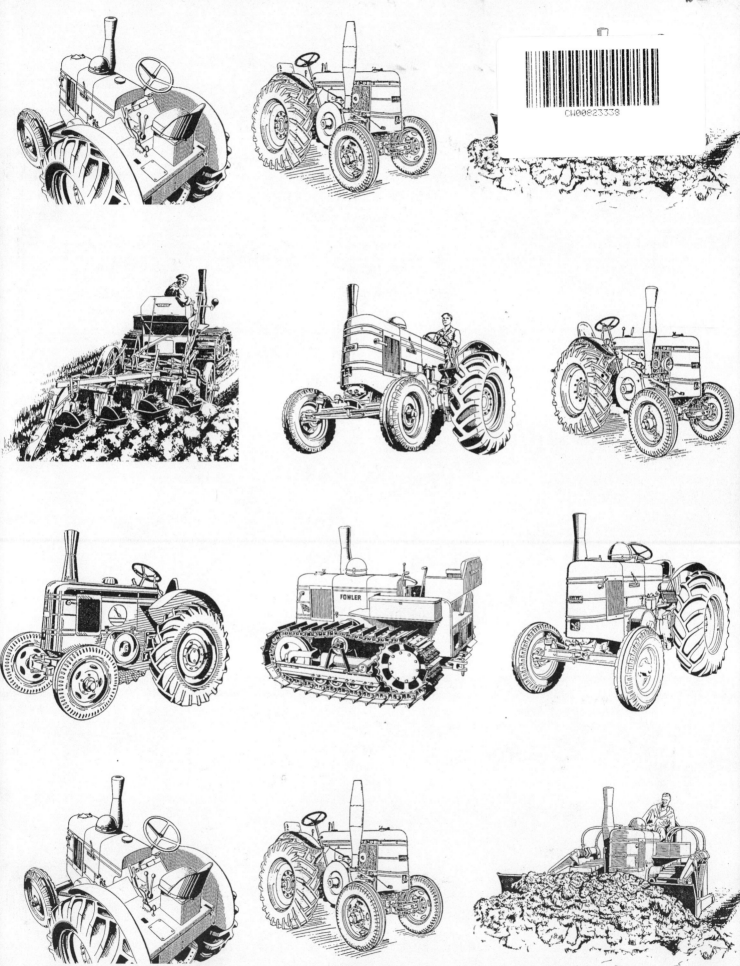

Glenshaw from Lew before Christmas 2002

Glenshaw from Lew before Christmas 2002

Three Decades Of
MARSHALL TRACTORS

Three Decades of
MARSHALL
TRACTORS

Peter Anderson

FARMING PRESS

ISBN 0 85236 380 X

A catalogue record for this book is available from the British Library

Published by Farming Press
Miller Freeman Plc
Wharfedale Road, Ipswich IP1 4LG, United Kingdom

Distributed in North America
by Diamond Farm Enterprises,
Box 537, Alexandria Bay, NY 13607, USA

Frontispiece

MP6 pre-production tractor no 6520002 on demonstration

near Roysden in Hertfordshire in 1957

Cover design and book layout by Hannah Berridge

Typeset by Winsor Clarke

Printed and bound in Great Britain by Jarrold Book Printing, Thetford, U.K.

Contents

Acknowledgments

The compilation of this book could not have been achieved without the kind help and assistance of a number of people.

Firstly I would like to thank Sharon Harvey, who cleverly deciphered my hand-written scrawl and converted it into a flowing and readable text. I owe a special thank you to Catherine, my girlfriend. She not only put up with my absence when I was fully tuned in to Marshall tractors but also helped me to edit and piece together each chapter.

Not forgetting my mother, who allowed me to use her home as a part-time office. She allowed me to continue writing without disturbance and provided me with endless cups of tea and Sunday roast dinners that were much appreciated.

I have certainly made many friends and acquaintances during my lengthy research. Many of these people, to whom I was a stranger, permitted me to continually bombard them with questions and to borrow treasured photographs.

Sadly, during the preparation of this book, one of the main contributors and a dear friend, Major Henry Marshall, passed away. Henry was a great inspiration. Although his knowledge of Marshall tractors was perhaps a little marginal, he pursued every problem I put before him and often provided the answers.

I was most fortunate to meet a number of ex-Marshall employees who were willing to provide first-hand information, sharing their years of experience as well as many fond memories. It was indeed a great pleasure to meet each and every one of them. I must say a special thank you to Sid Archer and Gerald Teft, for rallying around and finding former work colleagues to provide further resourceful information.

Special thanks also go to the following:
D Barrow, J Bloom, R Bramham (Track Marshall of Gainsborough), J Brown (Reading University) R Day, V Dodge, Gainsborough & District Heritage Association, S Gibbard, S Harvey, A Holstead, M Kellington, N Kellington, P Love, D Palmer, C Payne, D Sidwells, J Stephenson, B Tidbury.

If I had to mention every single person who has contributed to this book it would surely involve writing another chapter. So I will take this opportunity to thank you all for your help and most importantly your enthusiasm.

Preface

My fascination with tractors developed at an early age. I was about five years old when I first encountered a Marshall tractor, and I can vividly recall watching it ploughing in the fields adjoining our garden. Perhaps that was the moment when the Marshall bug entered my bloodstream. It did not take full effect, however, until 1968, when at eight years old I became the proud joint owner with my brother of a 1948 Field Marshall series 2, a Christmas present from my mother and uncle. From then on my interest in Marshall tractors grew and grew, as I began to collect literature and photographs that now cover a range of over 60 years.

This wealth of information, combined with my mechanical knowledge of the Marshall tractor, prompted me to form a Marshall tractor owner's club. In September 1988, with the kind permission of the late Major Henry Marshall, the Field Marshall Tractor Club was formed with co-founder Wally Hawkins. Along with many other club activities, I provide the archive material for the club's quarterly newsletter, 'Britannia News'.

With the intention of compiling a book on Marshall tractors, I gathered photographs and factual information which highlighted the vast changes through their progressive development and throughout their most significant years. To gain accurate detail and obtain first-hand knowledge, I visited many of the men who had played a vital role in the production of Marshall tractors, in various capacities.

I was fortunate to meet the men who designed these tractors, the men who built and tested them but more importantly those who carried out the field service work. All of these fine men gladly shared their vast experience and were able to provide vital information for the compilation of this book.

I have tried to be as accurate as possible, aided by my archive documentation, to pinpoint specific detail and where possible have shown photographic evidence.

Although the book is titled *Three Decades of Marshall Tractors*, I thought it would be appropriate to continue the history of tractor production and use Chapter 12 as an epilogue to bring Marshall tractors from 1960 to the present.

I have included various adaptations of the Marshall single-cylinder diesel engine, including the stationary power units, road roller, dumper, locomotive and the Fowler VF crawler. The VF is initially introduced in Chapter 6 to enable me to explain the development of the Field Marshall series 3 tractor. I continue with the VF in Chapter 9, culminating with the introduction of the Fowler VFA and the Track Marshall crawler.

To help avoid any confusion that may arise with determining the particular model of Field Marshall tractor in Chapter 5, I will explain the variations. The Field Marshall series 2 replaced the Mark I in 1947. The standard agricultural tractor became the Mark I series 2, while the contractors version became the Mark II series 2. Particular attention must be paid to the model mark and series when reading this chapter, as it is easy to confuse the original contractors tractor (Mark II) with the series 2.

The vintage tractor movement today contains a strong following for Marshall tractors. Their popularity reflects the affection for these loveable machines. The pom-pom note of the exhaust pipe and the erratic bounce generated by the vibration of the engine single out the Marshall tractor from the majority.

One must take into consideration the fact that tractors seen in preservation today have served many hours of work and accordingly during their lifetime many have received new components to replace worn and damaged parts. Parts often encountered supersession, hence the large number of early tractors with later components. The exhaust pipe and wheels are both typical examples of change and can easily confuse those with a limited knowledge of Marshall tractors as to the identification of a particular model.

Many early examples of Marshall tractors remain with us today, having stood the test of time. A majority were fortunate to have retired into preservation, while others, especially in Third World countries, continue to provide loyal service.

Marshalls always strived to maintain superiority in the construction of their machinery, and the Marshall tractor is indeed a prime example of this. It is rightly justified to say, 'If it was built by Marshall, it was certainly made to last.'

PETER ANDERSON
Guildford, 1997

CHAPTER 1
The Early Years

Based in the small Lincolnshire town of Gainsborough from 1848, Marshall Sons & Company Ltd had proven remarkable success in the field of engineering. With their vast and highly skilled workforce, Marshalls took on many of the challenges put before them and more importantly succeeded. By the turn of the century they had earnt the reputation of being one of the world's leading manufacturers of steam traction engines, rollers and threshing machines. Although the company later diversified into other areas, such as the production of boilers and tea-making machinery, it was their excellence in the manufacture of portable and stationary steam engines that were required to power agricultural and industrial machinery which upheld their universal reputation.

The reign of the steam engine remained unchallenged until the arrival of the internal combustion engine. By the late 1860s several rather crude attempts had been made to produce a motor tractor and by 1900 many British and American companies had achieved success in this area. The ever-increasing presence on the market of the motor tractor simply emphasised that the age of steam was seriously in decline. The clear-cut advantages of the internal combustion engine, over the steam engine, set the seal on the latter's fate. An advantage of the motor tractor was that it did not require the vast quantities of water, coal or straw that were necessary for fuelling the steam engine.

Britain was relatively slow in accepting the change from steam to the internal combustion engine; hence Marshalls' home market was protected. Unfortunately, the same could not be said of the overseas market as there were huge geographical differences between Britain and abroad. The equipment needed for cultivation of the vast Australian and Canadian prairies weakened

Aerial photo of Marshall Sons & Company, Britannia Works, Gainsborough circa 1947 (S Archer)

Line drawing of Marshall portable steam engine, threshing machine and elevator circa 1870

Typical Marshall 6 h.p. general purpose traction engine circa 1926

Marshall steam road roller circa 1926

Prototype 30 h.p. Marshall oil tractor on test at Bransby Farm nr. Gainsborough in 1906

Marshall 35 h.p. Class A oil tractor, threshing in southern Ireland in 1911

Marshalls' reputation in these areas. It became apparent that there was a preferred and cost-effective way to plough such huge tracts of land. Several American companies manufactured tractors specifically designed for use on the prairies, and these were large and powerful machines which were able to haul a 10-furrow plough.

Faced with such competition, Marshalls could no longer afford to overlook the situation. By late 1904 the fall in overseas sales became so marked that it necessitated a radical rethink. The following year Marshalls began to experiment with producing their own motor tractor, powered by a 30 h.p. twin-cylinder petrol/paraffin engine. After improvements and exhaustive tests, Marshalls introduced the prototype to the public and demonstrated that its abilities easily matched those of its American rivals.

Encouraged by their first experience into motor tractor production, Marshalls concentrated on manufacturing a range of tractors that could cater for the overseas market and so regained their dwindling foothold abroad. Since these tractors were designed with the colonies in mind, Marshalls aptly named them the colonial range.

This consisted of five tractors, which ranged from 16 to 32 h.p. (the horsepower rating as per steam engine and not equivalent to that which we use today). These tractors bore a strong resemblance to their American counterparts, with huge rear wheels and a large funnel at the front above the radiator.

The Marshall colonial tractors went on to win prizes at various demonstrations and tractor trials. They competed against some of the largest, well-established American firms such as Case, Avery and Rumley, with outstanding results. The degree of success Marshalls had, in their venture into the internal combustion world, was shown by the fact that by the end of 1914 over 300 units had been produced. Apart from serving in Australia and Canada, the range was also despatched to Africa, India and Iran, as all countries with large land mass benefited from the special design of these huge monsters. From commencement of production, overseas sales were consistently high. It is likely that they would have remained so, had it not been for the onset of the First World War, which caused production to cease. Government directives meant that Marshalls had to fully concentrate upon manufacturing traction engines,

Marshall 32 h.p. Class F colonial tractor circa 1910

threshing machines and elevators, which were required to maintain an adequate food supply for the country. In late 1914, the last batch of colonial tractors were exported to Russia and production never recommenced.

During the war years, over 2000 Marshall employees enlisted, which resulted in a reduction in the skilled workforce. Marshalls were not alone in suffering with a decimated workforce, as the cause was nation-wide. The loss of farm workers who had enlisted and the huge toll of human life on the battlefields led to an unprecedented labour shortfall. Ironically this meant that the Government wanted to exploit the use of the motor tractor, since it only required one person for operation, and increased levels of food production were of the greatest importance. Unfortunately, Britain could only boast a handful of tractor manufacturers and simply did not have the resources, facilities or mass production knowledge to fulfil the demand. The Government turned to the United States, placing many orders with American companies that had long mastered the skills and techniques required for mass production. A large number of American-made tractors flooded into Britain. In 1917 alone,

Henry Ford exported 7000 to Britain.

Although the First World War only lasted four years, that duration was costly not only in loss of life but in economic terms too. By 1918, Britain was caught in the recession seeping throughout Europe. Money was generally scarce and there was little spare cash in the Marshall coffers to enable them to continue with developmental ideas started before the war. Since Marshalls were reluctant to put money into further motor engine research, they reverted to concentrating on the steam engine, from the end of the war to the mid 1920s.

However, the age of steam, for traction purposes, was very much in decline, and Marshalls failed to recognise this. Always a little slow to adapt to change, Marshalls finally had to admit that they could no longer depend on their excellent reputation to boost the sales of steam engines. Times had changed and the British farming community wanted a modern, clean and efficient machine. Marshalls either had to adapt and give customers what they wanted or face the prospect of closure. Seeing motor tractors in the fields and farmlands of Britain, mostly American-made ones, simply added insult to injury. Other British companies had made incursions into the motor tractor trade in the immediate post-war years. By 1927, faced with ever-decreasing sales of steam engines, Marshalls recognised that their future lay with the motorised engine. A decision was taken by the Board of Directors to recommence motor tractor production and a specific proviso was set out. All efforts were concentrated to produce a tractor especially suited for the home market, rather than specialised ones for overseas use. Marshalls realised that they had to regain their foothold at home before they could consider expanding into the export market. They were already facing stiff competition from some European manufacturers, not to mention the continued presence of American-made machines.

It proved to be rather fortunate that Marshalls delayed returning to tractor production, as the time lapse worked in their favour, giving them the opportunity to study and glean ideas from their competitors' models. Marshalls were renowned for building machinery which was fairly simple in construction and had a good life expectancy. They had always adopted a policy of minimising the number of moving parts, for this led to

simplicity and cost effectiveness in the production stage and lessened the need for component replacement later. With the need for as much streamlining as possible, it was little wonder that Marshalls' attention was directed towards Europe, where some manufacturers had experimented with an alternative design of engine.

The motor tractor was usually powered by a conventional vertical 4-cylinder, petrol/paraffin, spark ignition engine. This was not only high in fuel consumption but temperamental in damp or wet weather; it also had an abundance of moving parts. The crude oil (or compression ignition) engine had been mainly used as a form of stationary power unit to generate power for industry. Its use became common in shipping, where it was a timely replacement for the old steam ships and barges. The design of the oil engine, in agriculture, was mainly of single-cylinder construction with two large flywheels. These not only provided the ability to drive machinery but kept the big single-cylinder engine in momentum. A compression ignition engine did not require a carburettor, spark plugs or magneto and simply

The Italian single-cylinder Bubba tractor, circa 1929 (note the striking resemblance to the Marshall 12/20 tractor)

The German-built Lanz horizontal single-cylinder crude oil tractor, 15/30 b.p.

relied upon a pump to distribute the fuel to an atomiser which then sprayed it onto the combustion chamber. Many of the earlier attempts to use this type of engine in tractors had been rather crude. Several were simply stationary units adapted and fitted onto a chassis with a chain-driven transmission. By the mid 1920s technology had advanced somewhat and there were a reasonable number of tractor manufacturers on the continent producing single-cylinder crude oil machines, a type rarely to be found in America. Manufacturers such as Orsi, Landini and Bubba of Italy; Hofherr-Schrantz-Clayton Shuttleworth (HSCS) of Hungary; and the two giant companies Mercedes Benz and Lanz of Germany were all successful in producing a single-cylinder tractor. Although Marshalls were impressed with all of them, it was Heinrich Lanz of Mannheim that influenced them the most.

The Lanz tractor was a 15/30 h.p. tractor, fitted with its own single-cylinder crude oil diesel engine. It had an immense 8⅞ in bore and 10¼ in

stroke, with a maximum speed of 500 r.p.m. It had the same starting technique as all the crude oil engines. Since these were of low compression, a hot bulb in the cylinder head at the front of the tractor had to be preheated using a blow lamp, which brought the temperature up to a level whereby the fuel could combust. The bulb was heated until it was cherry red, whereupon the engine would be primed and rocked to and fro until it fired. It would fire and run in either direction, with the blow lamp still in position, until sufficient heat had been generated by the engine to continue the cycle running in the normal fashion.

By 1927 Lanz had found distributors in London to sell their tractor to British outlets. The relative simplicity of its design, low fuel consumption and performance record intrigued Marshalls to the degree that they bought one, transported it to their Britannia Works in Gainsborough and stripped it to scrutinise its construction.

The late Major Henry Marshall on his 7 h.p. Marshall traction engine no. 45415, built in 1906, outside his favourite pub, The Beckett Arms, Corringham nr. Gainsborough 1989   (D Sidwells)

Marshall colonial tractor re-imported to Britain for preservation by the late Major Henry Marshall

From Prototype to Production

In 1928 the Board of Directors gave instructions to Marshalls' Chief Draughtsman, Sam Dawson, to commence drawings for a motor tractor based on the design principles of the Lanz tractor. Whilst Dawson concentrated on the design of the transmission, Jessie Lea was involved with the engine. Lea had been formerly employed by Davey Paxman Engines Ltd, a renowned engine firm in Colchester. His extensive knowledge proved to be extremely beneficial to his new employers, especially during the developmental stage of the prototype tractors and throughout the production of the later Field Marshalls.

The first tractor was assembled in the main erecting shops at Britannia Works where steam engines and rollers were in full production. Its general appearance was very crude, since it had no panelwork to cover the engine or rear wings.

Strangely, it did not match the Lanz tractor that had been studied in such detail but resembled the HSCS tractor manufactured in Hungary. Although influenced by the horizontal crude oil hot bulb engine, Marshalls chose to take their design a stage further and produced a tractor with a full diesel engine. Several disadvantages came to light with the hot bulb engine. Time was often wasted when starting these tractors with a blow lamp which entailed heating up the hot spot in the cylinder head. Often, in windy conditions, the lamp would go out, leaving the hot spot to cool. The inherent fire risk with this starting method was yet another disadvantage. The main benefit of the crude oil engine was that, as it was a low compression surface engine, it could use a variety of fuels. It could run on virtually anything that could pass through the injector and combust.

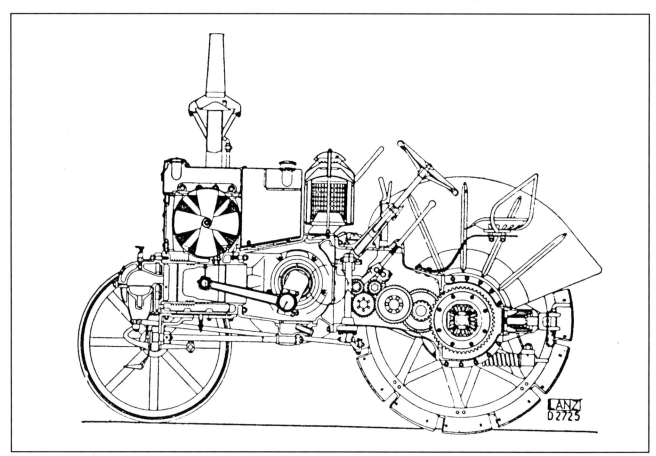

Sectional view of the Lanz Bulldog tractor produced in Mannheim, Germany. This particular tractor inspired Marshalls' developments in tractor design

First prototype Marshall single-cylinder diesel tractor in the traction engine erecting shop, Britannia Works 1928

Second Marshall prototype single-cylinder diesel tractor, driving a Marshall steel-framed threshing machine and straw buncher on wasteland nr. Britannia Works, Gainsborough 1929

The use of old engine oil, creosote, paint and even sunflower oil was not unheard of, especially in Third World countries where diesel supplies were limited. The crude oil engine was also prone to emitting large deposits of unburnt fuel, which the full diesel high compression engine did not do.

Several other British companies had already ventured into the use of the diesel engine for the agricultural tractor. Aveling & Porter, McLaren and Blackstone were firms similar to Marshalls, which had been renowned steam traction engine manufacturers and were keen to establish a foothold in the tractor market due to dwindling sales. The machines they had produced and already placed on the market were of a conventional, multi-cylinder 4-stroke vertical build. Marshalls, on the other hand, wanted to retain the single-cylinder horizontal engine that was used in the Lanz, and they were greatly influenced by the construction of its 2-stroke engine. There were no valves or mechanical linkage; instead it had an exhaust and an inlet port built into the cylinder wall. It was this simplicity that Marshalls wanted to emulate.

The Marshall had a full diesel engine which required much more compression to compact the gases in the cylinder to point of combustion. The prototype Marshall featured an 8 in bore and $10^1/_2$ in stroke, with a compression ratio of $15^1/_2:1$, which was far higher than that of the Lanz engine at $6^1/_2:1$.

The sheer amount of compression in the Marshall engine would have rendered it impossible to pull over its compression stroke with the use of a starting handle. To overcome this the engine was started on half compression and to facilitate this a decompression device was incorporated into the system.

A cable attached to the decompression valve, situated in the cylinder head, would be activated when a small roller wheel was pulled into contact with the inner face of the flywheel. The engine would be cranked and the ratchet would gradually draw the wheel away from the face of the flywheel. At a specifically machined position, in the flywheel, the roller would be released at a stage when the engine was in half compression. With the piston halfway in bore, the arm would drop, releasing the cable and thus closing the decompression valve ready for ignition. The piston being in a half-charged position meant loss of volume in the cylinder, which had a knock-on effect of there not being enough heat to create the combustion required for ignition.

The problem of lost generated heat was overcome by the use of a smouldering piece of paper which was inserted into the combustion chamber. The paper was pre-dipped in potassium nitrate (saltpetre) enabling it to smoulder rather than burn. It was rolled into a cartridge shape and inserted into a special holder, which screwed into the breech in the cylinder head. This special cartridge holder, being secured only by a screw thread, made for easy removal and allowed the driver ample time to insert the handle and crank the engine into life. Once the engine had fired, it discharged the spent paper with the exhaust gases through the exhaust port. It would then automatically return to full compression and proceed to run in the normal manner. This method of starting remained with the single-cylinder tractor until its demise in 1957.

In conclusion, it was rather ambitious of Marshalls to branch out into a totally new design, which took the form of a full diesel 2-stroke engine. Lanz did not proceed into full diesel tractors until 1957. Only two prototypes were made during 1928 and 1929, and sadly little else is known about them. Marshalls did not manufacture these tractors for production, for it was only an exercise to ascertain their abilities in the development of full diesel machines. After completion of the tests, the prototypes were scrapped and their parts were used in the construction of the 15/30 (model E) tractor, which followed.

With all the fieldwork completed by 1929 and greatly encouraged by their experiments with the prototypes, Marshalls confidently moved on a stage further and commenced production of an agricultural tractor geared for commercial success. Assembly took place in part of the steam engine erection workshops, alongside traction engines and road rollers. The project was put in the hands of the Foreman, Sid Brundell, and two service engineers, Stan Smith and Dick Simons. Field tests took place at Bransby Farm, owned by the Marshall family, which was in the small village of Pilham, near Gainsborough.

This tractor was labelled the model E but was more commonly referred to as the 15/30 tractor. With a maximum output of 550 r.p.m. it delivered

Prototype model E 15/30 single-cylinder diesel tractor, Britannia Works 1930
(Rural History Centre, University of Reading)

15 b.h.p. at the drawbar and 30 b.h.p. from the belt drive pulley. It retained the same single-cylinder diesel engine, with an 8 in bore and 10$\frac{1}{2}$ in stroke. As with the prototypes, the very first 15/30 utilised the original lubrication system, which consisted of the ratchet lubricator generally used in Marshalls' steam engines. The 15/30 gradually evolved from the prototype and a new lubrication system was incorporated into the build. Although still using the conventional 2-stroke dry sump principle, the ratchet method was discontinued and replaced by a rotary plunger pump driven from the crankshaft. The oil pump took its supply of oil from a small reservoir located above the crankcase, with a separate back-up situated to the rear of the fuel tank. This back-up was provided to prevent tractors from running out of oil during prolonged hours of work, and thus prevented damage to the engine. Used oil was not recycled into the lubrication

system at this stage, unlike the later Field Marshalls. It was pumped behind the flywheel through a sight glass and strained. The used oil would then be deposited into a separate sump under the crankcase, which would be periodically drained by opening a drain cock located at the bottom of the sump.

The starting technique was based on the same principle employed in the prototypes. The engine was cranked into life from the left-hand side, with the aid of the decompression valve and ignition paper. In cold conditions a priming cup, situated in the cylinder head, enabled the driver to insert light oil or paraffin into the combustion chamber. This increased the volume of compression and raised the temperature of combustion.

One of the greatest advantages of the Marshall diesel engine was in its starting technique. When the engine fired it continued to rotate in the same direction. The fuel injection system was timed so

An advert for the 15/30 tractor

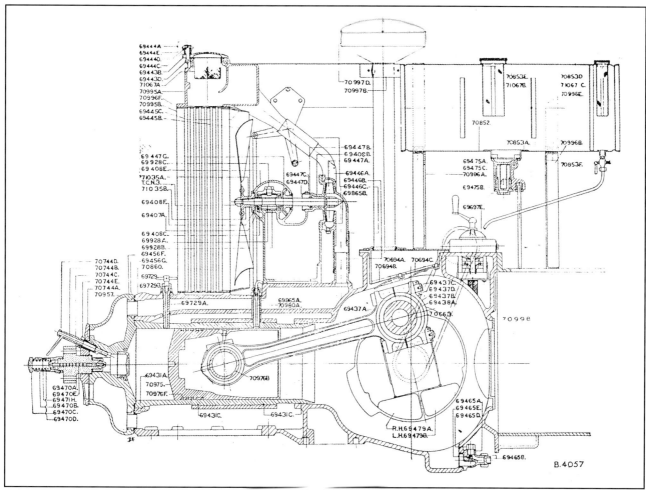

Marshall 15/30 tractor engine

that it would run clockwise rather than anti-clockwise. Along with many other makes of hot bulb engines, the Lanz could fire in both directions. Not only was this potentially dangerous but it also wasted time and energy if the engine failed to rotate in the correct direction first time, since it would then have to be stopped and restarted.

The cooling system consisted of a large radiator, mounted at the front end of the tractor, above the cylinder head. The water pump, driven by a belt via a worm wheel gearbox, helped circulate the vast amount of water (12 gallons) that was required for cooling the engine.

The power of the engine was transmitted to the gearbox through an asbestos-lined multi-plate clutch, located on the left-hand side of the machine. The gearbox had a selection of three speeds, three forward and a single reverse, giving a maximum of 5 m.p.h. in top gear and 1³⁄₄ m.p.h. in bottom. There were two types of brake power,

transmission and hand brake. The former was applied by fully depressing the clutch pedal and then bringing an arm in contact with the inner face of the flywheel, causing an immediate and effective brake to the transmission. The hand brake activated the rear axle and was generally used for parking, or for bringing the tractor to a graceful halt.

The model E made its first public appearance at the World Tractor Trials held at Wallingford in Oxford, on 2 June 1930, which gave Marshalls the chance to compete their new tractor against rival opposition. Weighing in at 6990 lb this sturdy tractor had sufficient weight to help it with adhesion and minimise wheel slip. On testing it performed considerably well, apart from a few minor setbacks with the fuel pump and a slipping clutch. Although out-performing many of the medium power petrol/paraffin tractors, the 15/30 struggled to compete against machines of a similar ability and construction. It was

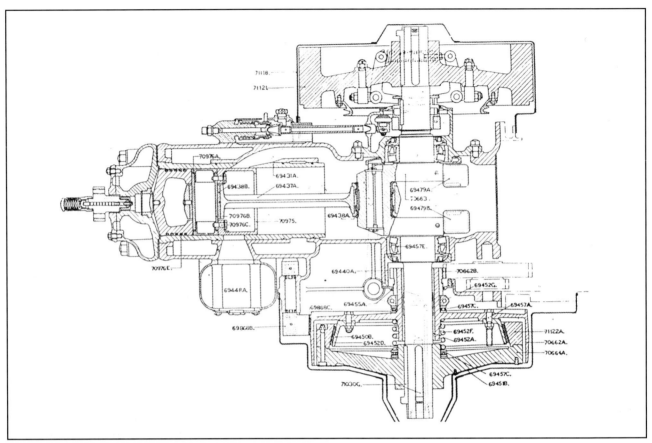

Top elevation of 15/30 engine

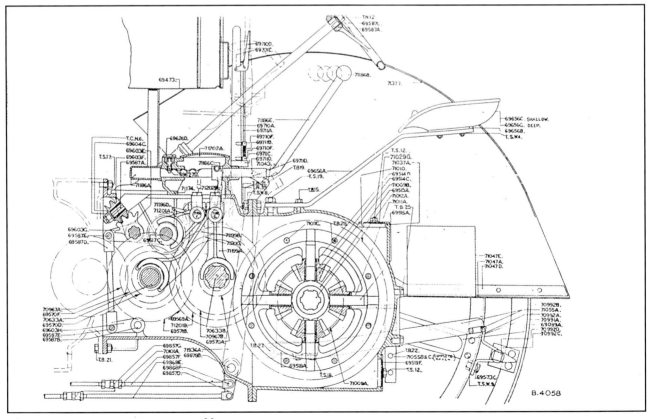

The 15/30 tractor transmission assembly

Model E 15/30 tractor taking part in the world agricultural tractor trials, held at Wallingford, Oxford in 1930

outstripped by the Lanz and HSCS tractors in power, although one consolation was that the Marshalls' fuel consumption could not be rivalled. It only consumed 1⅛ gallons of diesel per hour when engaged in heavy ploughing, compared to the 2¼ gallons that a petrol/paraffin tractor utilised. Marshalls were not disappointed with the performance of the model E. During testing it returned a maximum drawbar pull of 24.4 h.p. and delivered 29.1 h.p. on the belt pulley. This surpassed their own test ratings of 16 and 24 h.p. and prompted Marshalls into commencing full production.

Unfortunately Marshalls did not have the mass production facilities that were available in America, or in several large European companies; hence every 15/30 was erected on the shop floor by engineers and their apprentices. This allowed each tractor to be built according to the customer's requirements and many of the early 15/30s varied so much that there were rarely two alike. Adding to the individuality, the colour scheme was to the client's specification. Those unspecified were finished in battleship grey with red wheels. Many customers had their new machines finished in the same colour as their old faithful traction engines, which accounts for the number of 15/30s that were maroon. Customer

FROM THE 1930 WORLD TRACTOR TRIALS CATALOGUE
Selected Belt-test Reports
on Fuel Consumption

MAKE OF TRACTOR	LBS PER H.P. HOUR
Paraffin	
International 10/20	0.89
International 15/30	0.73
Peter Brotherhood	0.97
Vickers	0.85
Massey Harris 12/20	0.73
Case C	0.73
Fordson	0.84
Austin	1.02
Semi-diesel (crude oil)	
Lanz	0.74
Munktells 15/22	0.71
Munktells 20/30	0.68
HSCS	0.64
Diesel	
Blackstone	0.52
Mercedes Benz	0.52
McLaren	0.57
Aveling & Porter	0.55
Marshall 15/30	0.50

Model E 15/30 fitted with experimental Goodyear pneumatic wheels and tyres

loyalty apart, it was said that the men who had built the traction engines at Britannia Works would not allow the Britannia emblem to be fitted to motor tractors.

Compared to the average petrol/paraffin tractor, the model E carried a comparatively heavy price tag. In 1930 the price of a 15/30 on spade lugg wheels was £315, whereas at the same time on the market the mass-produced Fordson retailed at a mere £150. The Lanz was selling at £325, which reflected import costs, so the Marshall was at least cheaper than the German machine. The cost of the 15/30 was pitched as low as possible, to help fight off competition; Marshalls could not afford to reduce the price any further. The first run of 15/30s was built at a loss, which necessitated a cost-cutting policy. Marshalls targeted the high cost of manufacturing materials and strove to reduce the amount used.

The sheet metal used to build the mud guards and panelwork was originally $\frac{1}{8}$ in steel plate but was later reduced to $\frac{1}{6}$ in. The engine side panels were discontinued, which enabled a saving on materials, gave greater ventilation and also improved the cooling efficiency of the engine.

The length of the exhaust pipe was reduced by 2 ft, which brought the pipe a fraction above radiator level. The closer the pipe came to the radiator, the more the exhaust had to be angled away at the top, so as to prevent gases from entering the air intake and discolouring of the radiator header tank. Another change was replacement of the multi-plate clutch with a spring-assisted cone clutch, since the former developed a record for failing in service. Marshalls continued with this new specification for the rest of the 15/30's production.

In addition to catering for the agricultural market, the 15/30 was also adapted for industrial use with a sprung front axle, a down-swept exhaust pipe, lighting and a horn. The conventional spade lugg wheels were replaced by solid rubber tyre wheels, with which the tractor could be used in goods yards and factories for general haulage. One of these 15/30 industrial tractors was used by Marshalls in their own factory for hauling castings and machined parts from Britannia Works to Trent & Carr House Works, situated on the border of the town. Another modification was for use of the engine as

Rear view of model E 15/30 industrial tractor

Model E 15/30 industrial tractor with Marshall drilling rig

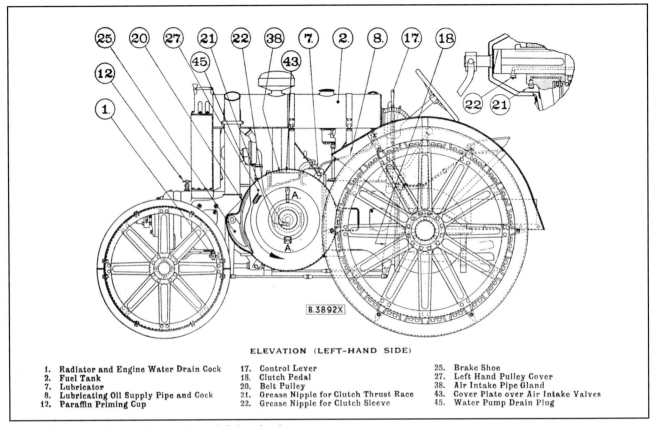

ELEVATION (LEFT-HAND SIDE)

1. Radiator and Engine Water Drain Cock
2. Fuel Tank
7. Lubricator
8. Lubricating Oil Supply Pipe and Cock
12. Paraffin Priming Cup

17. Control Lever
18. Clutch Pedal
20. Belt Pulley
21. Grease Nipple for Clutch Thrust Race
22. Grease Nipple for Clutch Sleeve

25. Brake Shoe
27. Left Hand Pulley Cover
38. Air Intake Pipe Gland
43. Cover Plate over Air Intake Valves
45. Water Pump Drain Plug

The 15/30 Marshall model E view from left-hand side

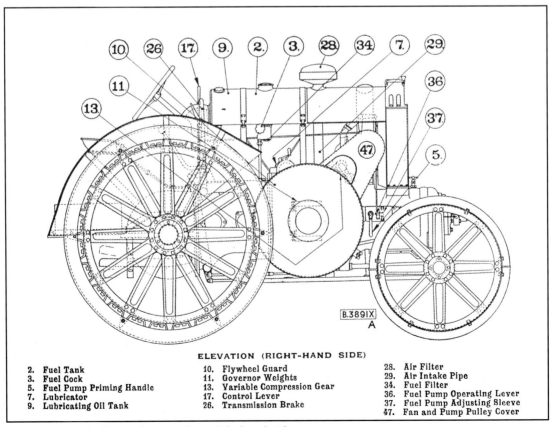

ELEVATION (RIGHT-HAND SIDE)

2. Fuel Tank
3. Fuel Cock
5. Fuel Pump Priming Handle
7. Lubricator
9. Lubricating Oil Tank

10. Flywheel Guard
11. Governor Weights
13. Variable Compression Gear
17. Control Lever
26. Transmission Brake

28. Air Filter
29. Air Intake Pipe
34. Fuel Filter
36. Fuel Pump Operating Lever
37. Fuel Pump Adjusting Sleeve
47. Fan and Pump Pulley Cover

The 15/30 Marshall model E view from right-hand side

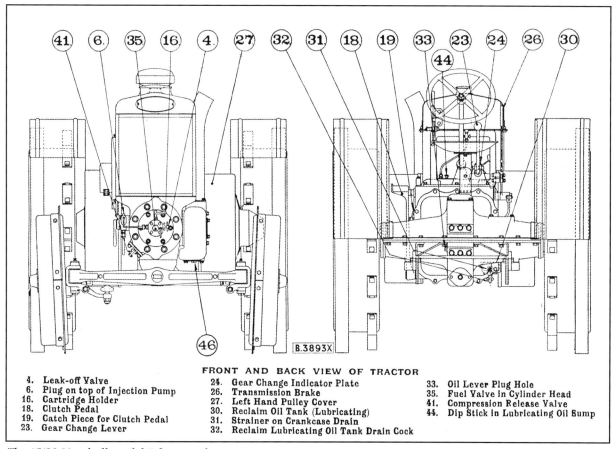

FRONT AND BACK VIEW OF TRACTOR

4. Leak-off Valve	24. Gear Change Indicator Plate	33. Oil Lever Plug Hole
6. Plug on top of Injection Pump	26. Transmission Brake	35. Fuel Valve in Cylinder Head
16. Cartridge Holder	27. Left Hand Pulley Cover	41. Compression Release Valve
18. Clutch Pedal	30. Reclaim Oil Tank (Lubricating)	44. Dip Stick in Lubricating Oil Sump
19. Catch Piece for Clutch Pedal	31. Strainer on Crankcase Drain	
23. Gear Change Lever	32. Reclaim Lubricating Oil Tank Drain Cock	

The 15/30 Marshall model E front and rear views

a stationary power unit. This was in principle the tractor with the transmission and front axle removed and was either mounted on a portable trolley or permanently housed on a concrete base. The 15/30, as a stationary power unit, sold at the relatively high price of £145. The availability of the well-established and proven stationary units by Lister, Petter, Hornsby and National at a lesser price meant that the 15/30 was not particularly successful in this area.

Several problems gradually came to light with the 15/30, during the early stages of production. In their haste to establish themselves in the motor tractor industry, Marshalls had not been as thorough in their field testing as perhaps they ought to have been. A common problem was the constant sticking of the fuel injection pump plunger, which was solved by removing the troublesome Marshall-built unit and replacing it with a Bosch pump. The gearbox selector forks and clutch linkage mechanism also regularly failed in service, as did the leather seals in the injection system, which was a particular problem in tractors working overseas in hot climates. All

these problems had to be ironed out, at the expense of Marshalls' profit sheet.

Many customers also complained of insufficient power and the inability to maintain power under constant load. Marshalls' solution was to call upon the services of Harry Ricardo, a leading engine development expert, who had vast experience with engine efficiency. His brief was to improve the power and efficiency of the engine, without any major structural alterations being made.

Ricardo's reputation was such that other manufacturers like McLaren, Paxman and Fowler had all previously enlisted his help. By 1931, Ricardo had boosted the Marshall engine's output by a further 3 h.p. by altering the exhaust and inlet ports, changing the fuel injection timing and reducing the weight of the flywheels. With this increase in power, Marshalls regained confidence and continued producing the 15/30 tractor to the new specification. Marshalls' advertisements, in the farming journals, noted the power increase to attract the home market but it was the overseas market which Marshalls wanted to concentrate on. Many 15/30s at that

Experimental 15/30 b.p. single-cylinder stationary power unit

time were despatched to Australia, Africa, Egypt, Belgium and Ireland. France was also targeted, and a large proportion of the orders for 1932 were distributed there. It was rumoured that one was sent to Russia, where it appeared at a large trade fair and starred amongst other products of the Marshall organisation.

Just when the order books were looking rather healthy, Marshalls suffered another setback. Reports came in that some tractors were having major failures with crankshafts cracking and structural cracks appearing around the crankcase and gearbox casings. Marshalls reacted by announcing a recall programme and many troublesome 15/30s were brought back to Britannia Works for a major overhaul. For problem tractors sold overseas, service engineers were sent out

from Gainsborough to rebuild them, sometimes in hostile and unpleasant conditions. In worst cases, the tractor was totally stripped down and refitted with a restructured engine casing and received a new erection number. Many of the offending 15/30s did not return to their owners in their original form. In 1932 when Marshalls were in the process of developing a re-styled and revamped 18/30 tractor, the recalled 15/30s left the works in a new guise with the 18/30 specification. Little is known about the total number of 15/30s produced as all records have been destroyed. From conversations with ex-Marshall employees, it is estimated that no more than 70 units were produced between 1930 and 1932, when the 18/30 came into being.

The only surviving Marshall 15/30 tractor model E

Marshall 18/30 tractor 1932

CHAPTER 3
Progress and Problems

The first batch of 18/30 tractors was rather mixed and consisted mainly of revamped 15/30 tractors that had been returned to the works and undergone extensive modification. Although records of the first 18/30s were destroyed, it is thought that production commenced around December 1932.* One record book survives, namely tractor erection book no. 2, which lists the machines produced between September 1933 and July 1937, accounting for 80 tractors. It is believed that the 60 18/30s constructed prior to September 1933 mainly consisted of revamped 15/30s. The 18/30 carried two numbers, one being an erection number and the other a plate

All Marshalls' records for 1936–57 except for Book 2 covering September 1933 to July 1937 were presumed destroyed in a fire in the factory premises in the late 1950s.

or serial number, and these were fitted after completion. Evidence of the integration of 15/30 and 18/30 tractors comes from noting the odd erection numbers entered in tractor erection book no. 2. Production of the first genuine 18/30 commenced at erection no. 309 with plate no. 530. Marshalls employed the tactic of jumping the plate numbers by three to confuse the opposition, but the erection numbers followed consecutively, except where a rebuilt 15/30 appeared.

The 18/30 had a different appearance from its predecessor. The square fuel tank and header tank had given way to an oval shape and the tinwork which surrounded the flywheels had to be slightly altered to accommodate this. This was a ploy by Marshalls to copy the shape of the very

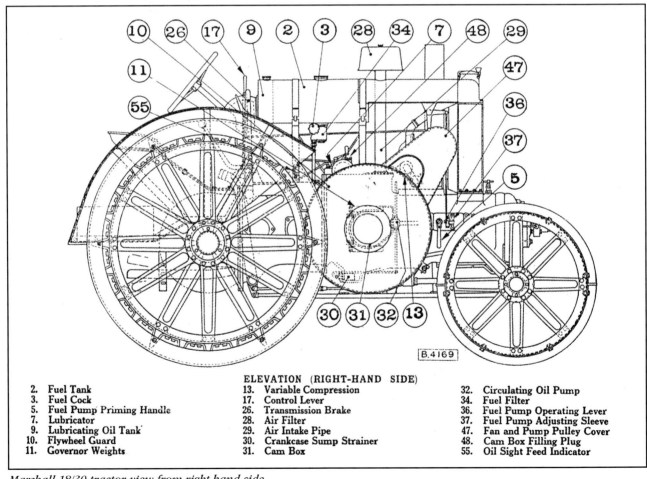

ELEVATION (RIGHT-HAND SIDE)

2. Fuel Tank	13. Variable Compression
3. Fuel Cock	17. Control Lever
5. Fuel Pump Priming Handle	26. Transmission Brake
7. Lubricator	28. Air Filter
9. Lubricating Oil Tank	29. Air Intake Pipe
10. Flywheel Guard	30. Crankcase Sump Strainer
11. Governor Weights	31. Cam Box

32. Circulating Oil Pump
34. Fuel Filter
36. Fuel Pump Operating Lever
37. Fuel Pump Adjusting Sleeve
47. Fan and Pump Pulley Cover
48. Cam Box Filling Plug
55. Oil Sight Feed Indicator

Marshall 18/30 tractor view from right-hand side

popular Fordson, which had become a familiar and well-established piece of farm machinery. During 1932 to 1937 when the 18/30 was in production, there were many variations in the tinwork covering the flywheels and rear wings, due to the availability of parts and the use of 15/30 spares. On all the 18/30s, the gear lever was moved from the right-hand side of the steering column to the left, due to modification of the gear selectors. Later models also featured a change in the position of the fuel control lever. Early models had the lever situated behind the fuel tank but it was later positioned on the right-hand side of the tractor. Another variance was that the exhaust pipe was straightened but this was still shorter than that of the prototype. The air filtration system also underwent a number of alterations, with early models fitted with the dry air filter element previously used in the 15/30. Later tractors were fitted with an oil bath air filter and the very last batch of 18/30s used the same enclosed fibre filter as for the 12/20 and model M tractors. Again the colour scheme was determined by the customer. Many tractors left the works finished in navy blue, grey or green, and the unspecified tractors were in gloss black with red wheels.

After 1934, the 18/30 was available with the option of pneumatic tyres. Although Marshalls' first attempts to fit pneumatic wheels to the 15/30 were unsuccessful, the 18/30 came with optional Firestone cast centred pneumatic rear wheels, and with a lighter pressed steel commercial front wheel to ease the ensuing steering difficulties. As

The Marshall 18/30 stationary power unit
(Rural History Centre, University of Reading)

An 18/30 in its industrial form

with the 15/30, however, cast wheel centres were unpopular because they added weight to a tractor already in excess of 3½ tons.

Like the 15/30, the 18/30 was made available with a number of adaptions for a variety of uses. The industrial version was much to the same specification as the 15/30 industrial model with the downswept exhaust pipe, electric lighting, hooter and solid rubber tyres. A T30 power unit was also produced using the engine from the 18/30, by increasing the size of the drive pulley.

Additionally, in late 1933, a crawler version became available, which used tracks and running gear supplied by Roadless Traction Ltd of Hounslow in Middlesex. Early models of the 18/30 crawler still retained the steering wheel and employed an elaborate mechanism to operate the slewing brakes, although later models had conventional brake levers. Existing records show that two 18/30 tractors received the Roadless track conversion. The first one received tractor erection no. 288 with plate no. 596 and was supplied to Robert Crawford of Boston, Lincolnshire, in March 1934. The other, tractor erection no. 339 with plate no. 668, was delivered to Roadless Traction on 3 September 1934. These were both late-build 18/30s and

hence featured the late specifications, including the enclosed fibre air filter assembly. There are no other records to refer to but photographic evidence exists of further crawler conversions. The tractor erection book also lists six tractors supplied to J Allen Oxford, in late 1933 and January 1934. Allen Oxford was not a Marshall distributor but an agent for Roadless. It is possible, although not recorded, that these six tractors were Roadless conversions. Close inspection of early crawler photographs shows that it had a steering wheel as opposed to slewing brakes. Evidently this tractor received the 15/30 shape exhaust pipe and could easily have been one of the 60 tractors that were in tractor erection book no. 1 and was most likely a revamped 15/30.

The Roadless tracks increased the weight of the crawler tractor, adding an extra 1½ tons to make the total weight a staggering 5 tons. Without the Roadless track conversion, in its standard spade lugg wheel form, the 18/30 was still far too heavy to be practical and Marshalls remained disappointed with the sales figures.

There was also an 18/30 contractors model designed for the threshing contractor, who used the power of the steam traction engines to haul

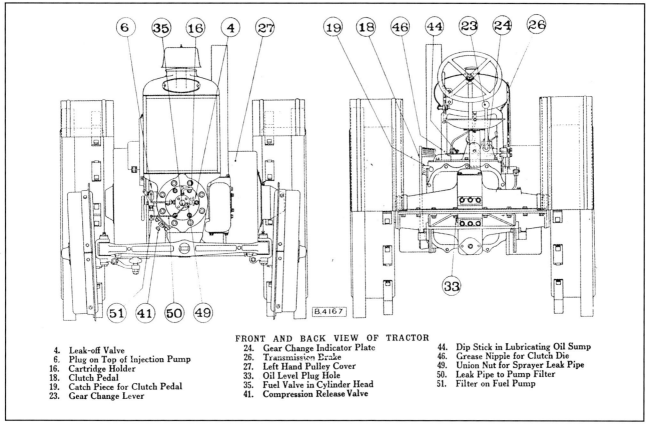

FRONT AND BACK VIEW OF TRACTOR

4. Leak-off Valve	24. Gear Change Indicator Plate	44. Dip Stick in Lubricating Oil Sump
6. Plug on Top of Injection Pump	26. Transmission Brake	46. Grease Nipple for Clutch Die
16. Cartridge Holder	27. Left Hand Pulley Cover	49. Union Nut for Sprayer Leak Pipe
18. Clutch Pedal	33. Oil Level Plug Hole	50. Leak Pipe to Pump Filter
19. Catch Piece for Clutch Pedal	35. Fuel Valve in Cylinder Head	51. Filter on Fuel Pump
23. Gear Change Lever	41. Compression Release Valve	

Marshall 18/30 tractor front and rear views

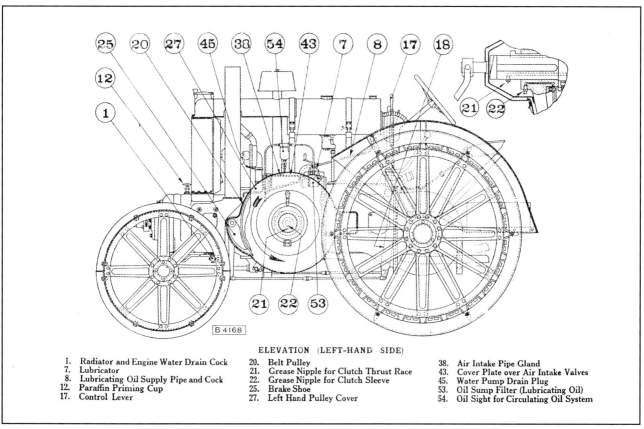

ELEVATION (LEFT-HAND SIDE)

1. Radiator and Engine Water Drain Cock	20. Belt Pulley	38. Air Intake Pipe Gland
7. Lubricator	21. Grease Nipple for Clutch Thrust Race	43. Cover Plate over Air Intake Valves
8. Lubricating Oil Supply Pipe and Cock	22. Grease Nipple for Clutch Sleeve	45. Water Pump Drain Plug
12. Paraffin Priming Cup	25. Brake Shoe	53. Oil Sump Filter (Lubricating Oil)
17. Control Lever	27. Left Hand Pulley Cover	54. Oil Sight for Circulating Oil System

Marshall 18/30 tractor view from left-hand side

A typical example of badge engineering: an 18/30 tractor on Roadless tracks exported under the Clayton badge

their equipment from farm to farm and to drive their threshing machines, balers and elevators. The contractors model featured a rear mounted winch, which could haul a load that was beyond the capabilities of the standard 18/30 drawbar. The winch had a single speed drum, which carried 50 yd of ⅝ in wire rope, with a mean line pull of 6000 lb. Although the winch was built by Marshalls, it is believed that Hesford Ltd of Ormskirk in Lancashire, who were leading winch manufacturers, played a role in the development of the winch drum and gearbox. Standard equipment on the contractors model included extra wide wheels to evenly distribute the weight and two sets of paddles which attached to the rear wheels when working in adverse conditions. A belt-carrying roller was fitted to the front wheel axle to prevent the belt from dragging when slack and thus fouling the axle.

Several attempts were made to boost the sales of the 18/30. Sales literature was distributed world-wide but this was not effective in gaining new customers. Marshalls had acquired the renowned Clayton Shuttleworth company in 1930. They had been rival steam engine manufacturers in Gainsborough since 1841 and, more importantly, held export licences for countries that Marshalls themselves did not have. The acquisition of this company gave Marshalls the opportunity to trade in areas which had been closed to them. Simply by substituting the Clayton badge for Marshall ones, a new sales area was opened and many 18/30s left the works destined for Belgium and Greece, under the Clayton Shuttleworth banner. None of the 15/30s went abroad under the auspices of Clayton Shuttleworth, probably as there were fewer of them produced than the 18/30, but the later 12/20 tractor was distributed under the Clayton badge.

Although most of the problems with the 18/30 were ironed out, this tractor still remained unpopular for a number of reasons. Feedback from Marshall agents consisted of complaints that the 18/30's performance record was inadequate.

Assembly of the 18/30, aided by overhead gantries in 1933, the early stages of assembly

Assembly line for the 18/30 tractor in 1933, nearing completion
(Rural History Centre, University of Reading)

An 18/30 contractors model complete with rear mounted winch

It was the machine's excessive weight that was a causal factor when sinking in light soil and compacting the ground. The unfavourable high price did little to whet the customer's appetite. In 1932 the price of a standard tractor on spade lugg wheels was £360, and for the same money one could buy two Fordsons with enough change to also purchase a suitable implement.

Marshalls refused to abandon the simple single-cylinder tractor by changing to a multi-cylinder engine and were confident that they were moving in the right direction. The 18/30 had at least proved to be economical to run and relatively easy to maintain. Marshalls concentrated on giving their tractor some major changes and a reduction in its size; hence its weight was the first objective. In 1933 the Development Department commenced work, designing a machine which incorporated the 18/30's character but which would also fulfil the requirements as identified by customer research. The Board of Directors gave specific instructions that the new tractor could not exceed the dimensions of the Fordson in height and length. They also decreed that the new machine was to fall in line with the increasingly popular medium sector of the tractor market.

The Development Department travelled extensively around the continent to study the machines on the European market, especially in France and Italy, and the new Marshall tractor was finally completed in February 1934. It still retained the horizontal 2-stroke diesel engine but had been totally reconstructed. The steering wheel, exhaust pipe and wheels were the only interchangeable parts with the former 18/30. The transmission and crankcase casing were of one solid cast construction, with the block and cylinder head built separately and attached to the main structure by studs, for easy removal

Rear view of 18/30 contractors tractor showing detail of winch
(Rural History Centre, University of Reading)

Early 18/30 fitted with Roadless tracks at work at Bransby Farm, Pilham nr. Gainsborough in 1933

Right-hand side view of prototype 12/20 tractor

Left-hand side of prototype 12/20 (note the oil reservoir mounted to the cylinder block, behind the front wheel)

during servicing. The size of the bore was reduced to 6½ in and the stroke to 9 in, and these dimensions remained unchanged throughout the life of the Marshall single-cylinder engine until 1957 when production ceased. With maximum revs at 600 r.p.m. the tractor delivered 10 h.p. at the drawbar and 20 h.p. from the belt pulley. The engineers found that by increasing the fuel injection pressures and altering the timing, the engine could safely produce a further 2 h.p. The model was aptly named the 12/20.

The air filter was based on the oil bath principle with the intake prominently positioned on the left-hand side of the tractor, above the clutch pulley. The engine still employed the same lubrication system as the 18/30, except that the old oil was delivered with the aid of crankcase pressure to a reservoir which was mounted on the cylinder block, on the left-hand side of the tractor. The cooling system saw a total change in design, as the 12/20 relied on the thermos siphon principle, without the assistance of a water pump. It was this new system that changed the appearance of the 12/20 so radically from that of

the 15/30 and 18/30 models. The radiators were transversely mounted either side of the tractor, above the cylinder block. A large belt-driven fan was situated between the sections which drew in air from the left-hand side and expelled it from the right. This cooling system was favoured by European manufacturers and the new 12/20 showed a strong resemblance to the Lanz tractor.

The starting technique was the same as with the 18/30, except that the engine was cranked from the right-hand side and was directed anti-clockwise. This change in rotation was due to a reduction in the number of shafts used in the transmission. The old ratchet decompression mechanism had given way to a much safer and less complicated system. This consisted of a disc being fitted to the decompression arm which, when engaged into the decompression position, would locate into a spiral groove that was machined onto the inner face of the flywheel. The engine could be cranked vigorously with the disc following the spiral groove until it left the flywheel, when the decompression valve would close with the piston in half compression for

Late-build 18/30 tractor (note the 12/20 type air filter assembly)
(Rural History Centre, University of Reading)

starting. The use of a transverse gearbox was still favoured in the 12/20 but only had two forward speeds and a single reverse.

A Ferodo-lined multi-spring cone clutch was again employed for separating the drive from the engine to the gearbox. This also incorporated the transmission brake, whereupon one depression of the clutch pedal would separate the cone and disconnect the drive. A further depression would bring the back of the clutch pulley into contact with two Ferodo blocks and act as a simple but effective transmission brake. The outer face conveniently provided a belt pulley with which to drive stationary machinery. The parking brake, when applied by means of a lever behind the fuel tank, expanded two oil immersed shoes inside a machined drum. These were located in the first speed gear wheel on the second motion shaft in the gearbox, and they not only acted as a parking brake but also as a powerful means of bringing the tractor to an abrupt halt.

Weighing in at 4700 lb with an overall length of 9 ft, the 12/20 was an ideal tractor for light duties and general farmwork. Only one prototype was produced, due to a severe cash-flow crisis within the company. The prototype was given erection no. 1 with plate no. 207, and most of the 12/20's field test work was carried out at the Marshall-owned Bransby Farm. The machine was sold to Mr Millegan of Stalham, in Norfolk, who was a friend of one of the directors and had always been a loyal customer of Marshalls machinery. It was sold with the proviso that Mr Millegan would agree to an evaluation programme, whereby engineers could periodically inspect and report upon the new tractor's performance. The prototype underwent several modifications during its working life in Norfolk, and was finally returned to Marshalls in 1938 to be scrapped. As a point of interest, Mr Millegan received a brand new 18/30 to replace the tried and tested 12/20.

Early example of a Marshall 18/30 tractor

Late-build 18/30 fitted with pneumatic tyres and Firestone wheel centres

Later example of an 18/30 with traction engine type canopy

CHAPTER 4
A Move in the Right Direction

With the feedback received from the field test engineers and also the driver of the prototype, Marshalls were able to ascertain both the abilities and the shortcomings of the 12/20. With all the field test data collated, it was felt that several modifications and additions should be executed. The second prototype was in preparation by November 1935, and although it remained fundamentally the same as the first, there were several alterations. One of the main changes required was the need for another speed in the gearing. The prototype, with only two forward speeds and a single reverse gear, could not offer the necessary range for general farm work. The oil bath air filter also proved to be troublesome, since it occasionally emitted dirty oil into the crankcase and contaminated the oil in the lubrication system. The exhaust also required an oil trap in the pipe to collect some of the oily smuts which found their way into the exhaust port. The prototype also had a tendency to suffer from lack of traction, due to the reduction of weight, and this was also targeted as an area for improvement.

In January 1936 Marshalls released the first of a line of tractors with the above modifications. The new 12/20 received a forward 3-speed gearbox which was carried out without any major structural changes, or the addition of further gear selection linkage.

Standard production 12/20 agricultural tractor circa 1936

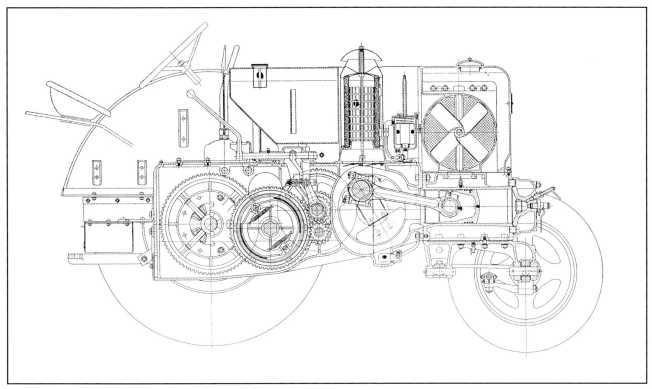

Sectional elevation of Marshall 12/20 tractor

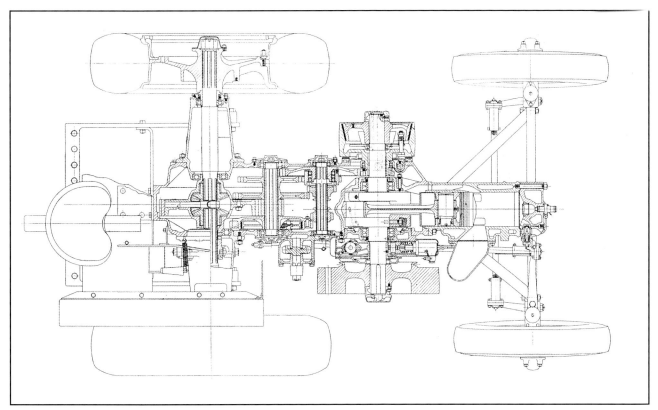

Top elevation of Marshall 12/20 tractor

These alterations were achieved by simply modifying the constant mesh first motion drive gear to incorporate a 3-speed gear. The second motion shaft gears were reduced in width to allow for the additional matching 3-speed gear, and by a slight alteration of the gear shaft gate the whole problem of a third gear was eliminated. The new 12/20 had a wider selection of gears to choose from, varying from 2, 3 and 4¼ m.p.h., with an optional 6 or 8 m.p.h., or a special high speed road gear of 15 m.p.h., available according to the customer's requirements.

The troublesome oil bath air filter was replaced by a dry (coconut) fibre filter. This was far more successful and appeared on late-build 18/30 tractors that were in production at the same time. This system remained in use in the Marshall single-cylinder engines until it was replaced by a fabric filter on the series 3A in 1953.

The exhaust system was also revised. The exhaust pipe was redesigned to incorporate a silencer and an oil catcher to accumulate the waste oil that found its way into the exhaust port. This captured oil was then expelled through a drain pipe onto the ground away from the driver. This did not eliminate the oily deposits but served to reduce them and was therefore a fraction cleaner on the driver's face.

Although the lubrication system had also been targeted for improvements, it remained much the same. The external reservoir which had been mounted on the left-hand side of the cylinder block was discontinued in favour of the used oil re-entering the sump via a filter. The used oil then passed through a filter situated above the crankcase and with the aid of crankcase compression, via a non-return valve, the oil was deposited back in the sump and then went into circulation again. This reduced the number of times the oil level would need to be checked, with a period of six working hours being given as the maximum interval between dipping the oil. The raised casting on the left-hand side of the cylinder block, which held the old type reservoir, remained as part of the block casing until the demise of the model M tractor which followed.

Marshalls tackled the traction problem caused by the reduction of weight by employing a differential locking device. This was effected by fitting a sliding coupler onto the right-hand half shaft, which engaged into the differential when operated by a lever situated under the steering wheel. With the differential locked, both wheels were able to operate together, and this provided greater adhesion in soft or boggy ground.

The new tractor proudly displayed a fresh colour scheme, disregarding the battleship grey used in the prototype. Tinwork and castings were finished in Brooklands green, with silver wheels. Customers could still specify their own colours if they so wished.

On 31 January 1936, after having undergone routine test procedures, the second 12/20 erection no. 2 with plate no. 210 was sold to Triumph of France. This company had already submitted orders for the 18/30 that had been in production simultaneously with the 12/20.

During the development and production of the 12/20, Marshalls had undergone financial hardship, and as a result there was little spare cash to be spent on further research and development. Continued production of the 12/20 was suspended whilst the company concentrated on fulfilling further orders for the 18/30. The 18/30 was influenced by the work which took place on the 12/20, and many changes in late-build 18/30s bear witness to this. One example is the installation of the dry fibre air filter with its distinctive upside-down-saucer-shaped rain cap. Despite continual improvement, it was clear the days of the 18/30 were numbered. In 1935 production amounted to no more than 16 machines. Of these, two were for the home market, one was destined for South Africa and the remaining 13 were for Marshalls' largest customer for the 18/30, Triumph.

In March 1936, when Marshalls were threatened by the possibility of receivership, a controlling interest in the company was taken by Thos W Ward Ltd, a renowned iron manufacturing company in Sheffield in South Yorkshire. The new directorship renamed the firm Marshall Sons & Company (Successors) Ltd and immediately delved into its past achievements to see how they could build on them to create a more profitable company. It was decided that the production of motor road rollers and high speed diesel engines was to be prioritised and production of the 12/20 recommenced. In May 1936 a third tractor to the same specification as tractor no. 2 was built for further field test work and was later used as a demonstration tractor. This tractor was given

A 12/20 hauling sugar cane in the West Indies
(Rural History Centre, University of Reading)

erection no. 3 with plate no. 213 but it was not recorded in the tractor erection book. It was not sold out of the company and remained at Marshalls throughout its life. Confident with their new tractor's performance, Marshalls released details of the 12/20 to the press and duly featured advertisements in the farming press announcing the 12/20's arrival and extolling its virtues. The 12/20 was received with great interest and several orders were placed for it. Marshalls employed the same sales tactics as used for previous models. They emphasised the power, economic values, simplicity of minimal moving parts and proudly boasted that the 12/20 would use no more than a gallon of fuel per hour when engaged in the heaviest of duties.

With increasing orders, final production was underway, with each tractor built by apprentices and service engineers alongside the declining 18/30 assembly line. Production was very slow and as certain machine tools were not available, many of the finished surfaces were carried out by hand. This included finishing the gears and shafts in the transmission with only the use of a file. This task was usually given to young apprentices who would spend hour upon hour perfecting the

finished part. As orders for the 12/20 increased, it was decided to finalise production of the 18/30. Orders had dwindled to a minimum as a result of the tractor's inability to compete against the competition, and the interest shown in the new 12/20 had dealt the final blow. As a result, 1937 witnessed the production of the last two 18/30s, and erection no. 174 with plate no. 785 went to Triumph. Production of the 18/30 was finalised so that full production of the 12/20 could be concentrated upon.

The delay in the commencement of production of the 12/20 worked in Marshalls' favour, for it gave them a longer period of time in which to test their new tractor and to rectify any faults. The 12/20 was definitely a step in the right direction, and the future was looking far more promising, as Marshalls were faced with increasing orders for their latest machine.

The production 12/20s remained fundamentally the same as the third pre-production tractor. Due to the increasing popularity of the pneumatic tyre, the 12/20 had the option of Dunlop cast centred pneumatic wheels as opposed to the spade luggs. The front wheels were fitted with 600 in x 19 in closed centre tread

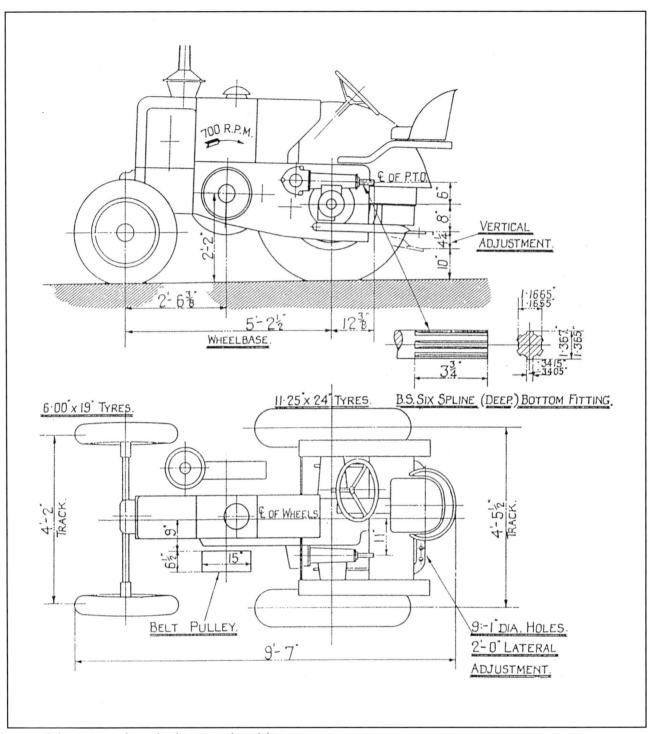

700 R.P.M.

℄ OF P.T.O.

VERTICAL ADJUSTMENT.

2'-2"

8" 5"

10" 4·4"

2'-6⅜"

5'-2½"

12⅜"

WHEELBASE.

1·1665"
1·1655"

3¾"

1·367
1·365"

·3415"
·3405"

B.S. SIX SPLINE (DEEP) BOTTOM FITTING.

6·00" x 19" TYRES.

11·25 x 24" TYRES.

4'-2" TRACK.

℄ OF WHEELS

9"

6½"

15"

BELT PULLEY.

9'-7"

4'-5½" TRACK.

1"

9:-1" DIA. HOLES.

2'-0" LATERAL ADJUSTMENT.

General dimensions of standard 12/20 and model M tractor

An unusual task for a 12/20, hauling a set of gang mowers on an English golf course

Medium duty winch fitted to a 12/20

tyres as standard. A further option of 12³/₄ in x 24 in balloon tyres was available at the customer's request. The use of pneumatic tyres on the 12/20 was certainly beneficial. They not only made the tractor more versatile but also helped absorb some of the vibration from the momentum of the single-cylinder engine. It was not surprising that more pneumatic wheeled tractors were sold than those with the spade lugg wheel standard fitment. The differential lock became an optional extra but very few tractors were sold without it because it was essential if the tractor was required to work in adverse conditions.

The 12/20 in its standard form was very basic and consisted of the bare necessities in order to keep the retail cost down, so as to be competitive in the market place. In 1936 the price of a 12/20 in its basic form with steel wheels was £285. This included a comprehensive set of spanners, grease gun, oil can, a small selection of small wearing parts, an instruction and parts manual and a tarpaulin sheet. This price was far more attractive than that of the 18/30, although it still could not compete with the mass-produced Fordson that

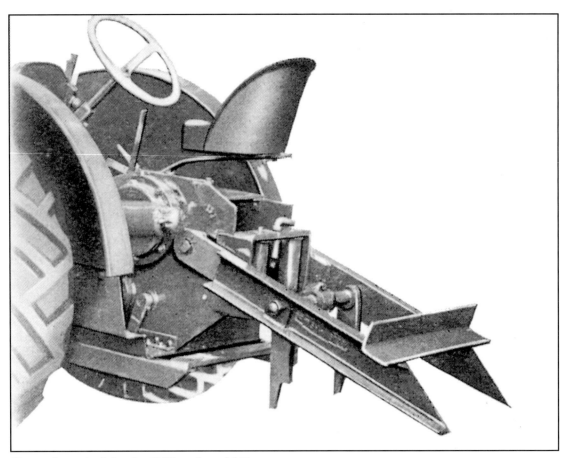

Heavy duty winch for the 12/20 and model M

was available on pneumatic wheels at a mere £175. This low price reflected that Fordson had taken advantage of the gap in the market way back in 1933, when they first set up mass production facilities in Dagenham. The only thing in Marshalls' favour was their reputation for reliability and simplicity of design, together with an unrivalled economic fuel consumption record.

Apart from the essential options such as the pneumatic wheels and differential lock, there were other accessories available which enhanced the tractor's abilities, more importantly the choice of two sizes of rear mounted winch. The availability of a winch was a vital factor in the ensuing success of the 12/20 and was popular amongst threshing contractors, for whom a winch was essential for hauling the heavy threshing outfit across the muddy fields and farmyards. This task was quite beyond the scope of a basic tractor's drawbar. Of the two winches made available, the smaller one was introduced first and was known as the medium winch. It was positioned neatly at the rear beneath the driver's seat and facilitated the positioning of the threshing outfit

once attached. It was ideal for general light work such as the removal of tree stumps and saplings.

The drive was taken from the optional implement power take-off shaft, which incorporated a dog clutch that could easily be disengaged after depressing the tractor's clutch pedal. The winch drum capacity had a standard fitting of 50 yd of $^7/_{16}$ in diameter wire rope and an option of 70 yd of $^3/_8$ in and 100 yd of $^5/_{16}$ in. The speed of the drum was controlled by the fuel control lever with a rope speed varying between 58 and 136 ft per minute. This produced a maximum mean line pull, exerted at the rope drum, which varied between 3500 and 4850 lb. The winch anchors were built of a heavy angle iron construction, positioned neatly beneath the drawbar and fitted with check chains to prevent the tractor overrunning the anchor when engaged in hauling a substantial load. Of the two winches the medium was more compact and much tidier in appearance.

The heavy duty winch was much sturdier than its counterpart, having been primarily designed for forestry, and was ideally suited to hauling

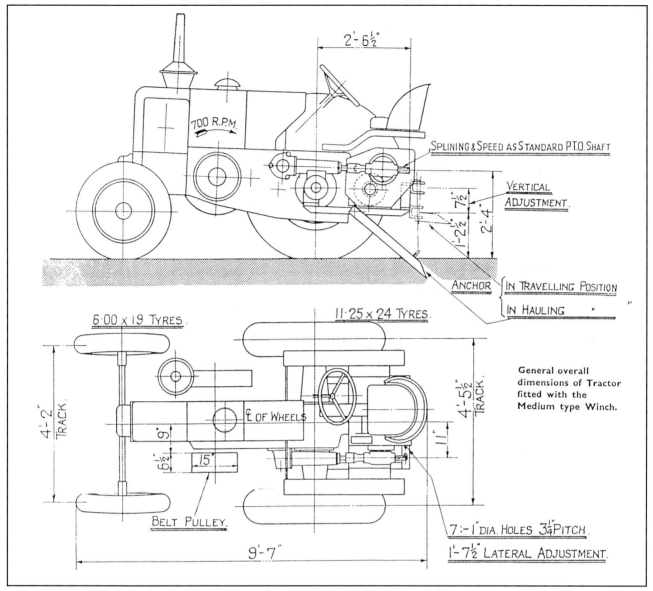

12/20 and model M, light duty winch

large trees and uprooting trunks. Being such a cumbersome addition, it gave the general appearance of a tractor fitted to a winch as opposed to a winch fitted to a tractor. Some large country estates purchased the 12/20 with heavy duty winch to help maintain the grounds.

The drive was again taken from the power take-off shaft but unlike the medium winch the heavy duty winch was unable to provide additional facility to power farm implements. It was decided that the 12/20, with its heavy duty winch, would mainly be marketed to the timber industry and would not need a power take-off shaft. This winch had far more to offer than the medium winch, as it provided a maximum mean line pull on the drum which varied between 5000

and 7000 lb and a rope speed between 38 and 90 ft per minute, determined by the speed of the engine.

To maintain the extra purchase this winch could supply, a much sturdier anchor frame was fitted with checks to prevent the tractor overrunning the anchor. A latch was provided that would hold the anchor in one of two positions when in transport. It was easy to recognise the heavy duty winch as the anchors stood out prominently at a 45 degree angle when in transportation. Early heavy duty winches used the same design of anchor fitted to the medium winch but this was soon discontinued in favour of the large winch anchor, as it was discovered that the tractor could be pulled over backwards with the extra load. Both heavy and medium duty

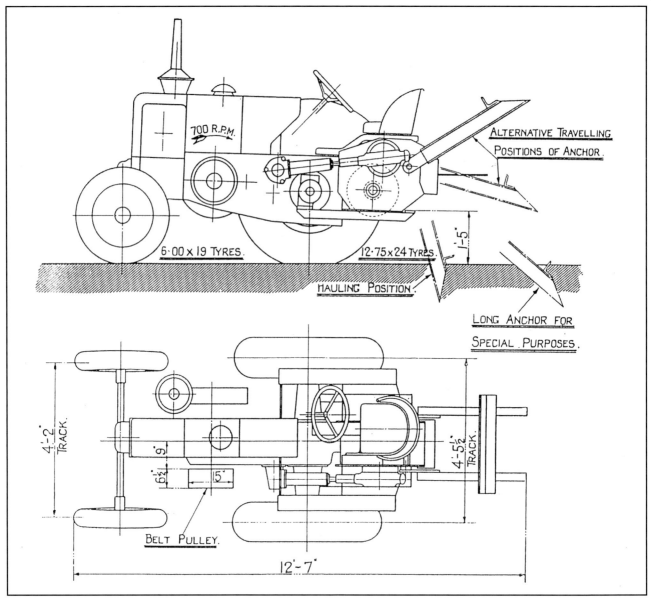

700 R.P.M.

6·00 × 19 TYRES.

12·75 × 24 TYRES.

ALTERNATIVE TRAVELLING
POSITIONS OF ANCHOR.

1·5

HAULING POSITION.

LONG ANCHOR FOR
SPECIAL PURPOSES.

4'-2 TRACK.

6½"

5"

9"

4'-5½" TRACK.

BELT PULLEY.

12'-7"

Heavy duty winch for the 12/20 and model M

winches had the option of a further rope guide roller, positioned beneath the winch, which enabled the driver to carry out winching duties from the front of the tractor. Also, weights could be bolted on the front wheels or front axle to compensate for the additional weight of the winches. Other optional equipment included a belt roller for the front axle, a chaff screen for the radiator and a 12 volt electric lighting set that comprised one rear light, two side lights and a work light positioned above the cylinder head. The dynamo took its drive via a belt fixed to a double pulley on the radiator cooling fan. A front drawbar hitch was also included as an optional item to the 12/20.

Hydraulic rear wheel brakes could be provided with special rear wheel centres made by Firestone Wheel & Tyre Company, which incorporated brake drums. The hydraulic brakes were favoured by the threshing contractors since they facilitated bringing the train of threshing machine, baler, elevator and living van to a halt. Optional 6 in steel overtyres for the spade lugg wheels enabled the tractor to be driven on the road, without causing damage to the surface or discomfort to the driver. There was also the option of a deeper spade lugg for traction in muddy conditions and a canopy to protect the driver from adverse weather, though this was not often fitted.

A 12/20 with the Clayton badge

A 12/20 working in Australia (note the wide wings and air filter extension pipe)

The 12/20 became a substitute for the steam traction engine. The versatility of this machine and the easily accessible belt pulley made it an ideal tractor for powering stationary machinery, capable of delivering a maximum belt speed of 2750 ft per minute at 700 r.p.m. The optional power take-off drive shaft provided a maximum speed of 538 r.p.m. and was capable of producing the power to drive most makes of power-driven farm implements, such as manure spreaders and finger mowers.

With many well-established Marshall distributors world-wide, the 12/20 was exported all over the globe. Though the European market was the strongest, it was sold to Australia, New Zealand, Africa, India, Canada and the West Indies. For those machines sold abroad to countries with a warmer or dustier environment than that of Britain, there were variations in the specification; wide rear wings and an air intake extension with pre-cleaner element became a standard feature. A small percentage of 12/20s left Britannia Works finished in the Clayton Shuttleworth livery in order to acquire sales in countries where Marshalls did not have a sales licence.

A number of leading tractor manufacturers had achieved further sales by recognising the niche in the market for specifically adapted tractors for industrial use. Where previously horses, then steam tractors, had been employed for shunting railway rolling stock, some prominent manufacturers began to produce specifically designed tractors. Marshalls, ever eager to improve sales figures, followed suit and made available a shunting tractor. It consisted of two 2 ft x 3 in lengths of channel iron mounted on each side of the tractor and secured to the front and rear axles. Two 2 ft 6 in deep x 6 ft wide buffer plates, attached to the channel iron frame, were positioned to the front and rear of the tractor with the provision of buffer plate couplings with which to hitch up to rolling stock. A 12/20 shunting tractor was used at Britannia Works for many years, replacing their outdated 18/30.

The forward-thinking Thos Ward company, who controlled Marshalls, inspired another variation of the 12/20. Since they were actively involved in the construction industry and in scrap

metal, they were aware that there was a high usage of dumper trucks in these areas. The majority of dumpers relied on a modified farm tractor to provide the power unit for the outfit. The Fordson tractor was the most popular, and Muir-Hill used Fordson skid units in the construction of their famous dump trucks. Thos Ward, not wanting to miss out on an opportunity to gain further success with the 12/20, approached the Board with the idea of manufacturing a dumper truck that incorporated the 12/20 tractor skid unit. Consequently, in April 1938, tractor erection no. 105 with plate no. 660 left Britannia Works in the form of a dumper.

Obviously a number of modifications had taken place. The direction of the engine's rotation was changed to give the correct direction of travel. This resulted in the driver being positioned in the opposite way, facing the 2½ cubic yd skip that was mounted on top of the gearbox housing. A downswept exhaust was also used and the whole engine was shielded by a bonnet with hinged doors. The new dumper was labelled the model A. Unfortunately, it did not meet expectations and although all records have been destroyed it is believed that no more than a mere 150 units were made. Contributing to its early demise was the weight factor. Weighing in at almost 3 tons did little for its ability to operate in the often boggy conditions of a building site and complaints were received about bogged-down units.

Also the position of the driver's platform on part of the channel iron chassis, on the clutch pulley side of the tractor, did little to help the

A 12/20 shunting tractor

Left-hand view of Marshall single-cylinder diesel dumper
(A Halstead)

Marshall T20 stationary power unit

cooling efficiency of the engine. The position of the footplate alongside the radiator section meant that mud accumulating on the platform, from the driver's boots, often clogged up the radiator and led to the engine overheating. Another factor contributing to the lack of success was the relatively high price of nearly £400 per unit, and only a handful of orders went to customers outside Thos Ward. Due to the poor performance rate, many model As were returned to Britannia Works and scrapped after only a very short term of service. The Marshall dumper has not yet found its way into the preservation world, fuelling the theory that every one of them was indeed scrapped. It continued to be produced until 1943, latterly using the model M tractor skid unit instead of the 12/20.

As an ambitious attempt to add to Marshalls' range of steam, oil and diesel powered stationary engines, the 12/20 power unit became available as a stationary engine. By simply recasting a new crankcase so that it did not incorporate the gearbox used in the tractor, the new diesel stationary engine called the T20 diesel power unit was produced. As the stationary power

4648

Marshall RC20 single-cylinder diesel road roller

unit did not require a clutch, the pulley was replaced by a flywheel. This incorporated a large driving pulley, with an outside diameter of 18 in and width of 11 in, that produced a belt speed of 3300 ft per minute and a variation of pulleys available on customer's request. In 1936 the price of a T20 unit was £145 when supplied on a concrete base. Marshalls did not recommend that the T20 be mounted on a portable trolley because of the vibration exerted when the engine was running. Though the T20 did not have good sales in its home country, it was more successful abroad. There was a greater need for units to power generators and irrigation pumps in countries such as Australia, New Zealand and Canada.

By the mid 1920s Marshalls had experimented with motor engines for their road rollers, using both petrol and oil engines to provide the power. Although steam had not met its end like the traction engine and the last steam road roller produced by Marshalls was as late as 1956, the use of steam was declining. Marshalls wished to include motor road rollers in their range. From a variety of engines available, Marshalls provided the T20 power unit in their RC series of rollers, produced from 1936 until 1945. Known as the RC20, this roller was available in eight different sizes ranging from 6 to 14 tons, each fitted with a full length canopy. The smaller rollers were provided with a 2-speed gearbox and the middle sector had the option of 2 or 4 speeds. The larger, which were 9 tons and above, were fitted with a 4-speed gearbox.

With the momentum from the single-cylinder engine, the RC20 could easily have been identified as one of the first vibrating road rollers, but it was the engine's vibration that led to its unpopularity. Operators often complained of the discomfort in using these rollers and another drawback was the tendency to sink into soft tarmac when the roller was left stationary. It is no surprise that multi-cylinder engines became the popular choice for the RC20 roller, and customers were even willing to put up with their high consumption of petrol. Marshalls bought in multi-cylinder engines, since this was more cost effective. Earlier rollers were fitted with a Ford 4-cylinder petrol/paraffin power unit while later ones were fitted with a 4-cylinder diesel engine, supplied by the famous Perkins Engine company. The Perkins engine remained with the Road Marshall range of road rollers until 1975. Marshalls were taken over by Leyland, from Lancashire, who were well established in the production of road-rolling machinery. Eventually Leyland phased out production of the Marshall road roller in favour of their own Aveling Barford range.

During the two years in which the 12/20 was in production, it was under constant development. Many improvements were effected, as a result of feedback from both customers and service engineers. Such improvements are evident in the construction of later-build tractors. For example, the height of the exhaust pipe was extended by 18 in so as to lessen the amount of smoke, sparks and oil in direct contact with the driver's face. Various major structural alterations were also made to the transmission housing by adding additional webs and braces, in order to gain extra strength in areas that had failed in service. The rear axle casing was prone to failure when fitted with the heavy duty winch, particularly if the operator had been working the outfit to the limits of its capabilities. The engine's output and performance were also improved by altering the fuel pump timing and increasing the compression. Along with the uprated performance, the main bearing housing was strengthened and the oil pump and feed pipes were modified to achieve an improved circulation of oil.

The Dunlop 24 in cast centre rear wheels, used in earlier 12/20 tractors, were discontinued and replaced by the Firestone 24 in cast centre wheel, which had a hub with ten studs which made it slightly easier to change a wheel. The specification was also slightly altered due to the increased popularity of the pneumatic tyre. Spade lugg wheels became optional extras and a basic tractor was supplied on 11¼ in x 24 in low pressure pneumatic rear tyres, with 600 in x 19 in front tyres as standard equipment. Further accessories included a front mounted drawbar hitch, a belt guide roller and for the devoted tractor owner a brass Marshall oval emblem in favour of the factory-fitted cast aluminium or iron badges.

Several minor changes followed in later 12/20s at random, including the provision of a cushioned upholstered seat and a fabricated

4-spoke steering wheel that superseded the cast aluminium 3-spoke wheel. There were no cut-in or cut-off points in serial numbers and the modifications were filtered through on an ad hoc basis. More often than not, if stocks of modified parts were exhausted, Marshalls would revert to using the former parts so as not to disrupt production.

Marshalls employed a clever tactic to bring all of these improvements to their customers' attention by renaming the 12/20 the new model M (medium tractor). It is not clear what serial number was given to the first model M. A 12/20 tractor, erection no. 180 with plate no. 798, was prepared to the model M specification and supplied to the Royal Agricultural Society of England, in Oxford on 19 September 1938 for tests. The report sheet refers to this tractor as the model M and so it would appear that this was the very first. During the test periods that began on 23 September and until the publication date of the report, several 12/20s would have been made, although not likely to the M's specification. To throw a little light on the ongoing question of the serial numbers indicating 12/20 and model M tractors, it can be taken for granted that any tractor with a serial number preceding 810 is not a model M, unless it was an earlier tractor that was returned to Marshalls for a major overhaul and then received a new serial number.

Allowing for this small area of doubt in the 12/20s and in integration figures, a total of 190 12/20 tractors were manufactured in the two short years of production. These figures clearly indicate the small volume of production, mainly due to a lack of facilities rather than of demand.

The model M, riding on the coat-tails of the success of its predecessor the 12/20, was met with an enthusiastic welcome. The Marshall single-cylinder tractor proved to be an ideal replacement for the steam traction engine. Again, the domination of the motor tractor over the steam traction engine continued. By the late 1940s, even those stalwarts for tradition, the threshing contractors, had been weaned away from their old outdated traction engines and had converted. The whiff of steam in the construction of the model M had made this defection all the easier.

At the outbreak of the Second World War in 1939, under Government directives Marshalls

Early model M ploughing in Yorkshire circa 1938

turned out a variety of weapons such as 4 in naval guns and midget submarines. Despite a reduced workforce, Marshalls were amazingly enough able to increase their output of tractors and threshing machinery. Due to the relatively small scale of agricultural machinery produced nationally, together with an ever-increasing demand for machines to make up for the shortfall in labour, Marshalls did not receive any sanctions restricting production levels. Eventually, production of the model M was disrupted because of the inevitable shortage of materials that ensued. In many cases a model M received some 12/20 parts, especially wheels and tyres, as these were the first items to go into short supply. The shortage of materials also meant a change from the use of brass for fuel and oil caps, as brass was more urgently required for making gunshell casings. Marshalls reverted back to the 15/30 and 18/30 filter cap design, which consisted of a flat plate lid secured by a screw thread knob.

It is true to say that very few of the model M tractors were identical. With the use of parts from the former 12/20, together with frequent changes of supplier, Marshalls continued to offer a personal service whereby customers' individual needs were catered for. All these factors meant that the model M was far from ever being standardised Incidences of component failure, increasing as a side-effect of the changes in suppliers, also meant that the model M underwent many alterations during its short life span.

One of the first alterations to come about was in 1939, when the hand priming handle on the oil pump was modified because of the problem of impurities entering the oil pump housing via the primary handle shaft. Model Ms built after serial no. 1003 received an enclosed priming shaft that was only accessible by removing a brass inspection plate, secured by two wing nuts. Also, in 1939 the steering ball joints were replaced by an adjustable joint which proved so successful it remained unchanged throughout the remaining life of the model M and continued to be used in the Field Marshall range.

To try to standardise outside supplies, the fuel filter housing, once supplied by Vokes of London, was replaced by a CAV filter. This unit was easier to maintain and dismantle with a screw plug at the top of the housing. The Vokes filter was more complex, and access to the filter element was only achievable after unscrewing a series of bolts. Another disadvantage was that even after regular service it would often leak fuel around the sealing joint. The Vokes filter was discontinued in favour of the CAV after serial no. 1017.

As a cost-saving exercise the oil pressure gauge was replaced after serial no. 1061 by an oil pressure button, which consisted of a plunger that rose with the oil pressure behind it and gave a clearer indication that the oil pump was working efficiently. The year 1941 saw further additions and modifications. The exhaust pipe received a coffee-pot-shaped extension to capture

Prototype model M tractor ploughing at Bransby Farm, nr. Gainsborough 1938

Marshall model M equipped with heavy duty winch, lights and driver's canopy

some of the oil deposits and to act as a spark deflector, though its actual effect is disputable. Also in 1941, optional 28 in Firestone cast rear wheels were introduced, which became standard after 1942. The change in the height of the wheels slightly altered the posture of the tractor. This was later found to cause a problem when driving belt-driven machinery with a high pulley, as the belt would become damaged as it fouled the clutch-operating linkage. This was overcome by simply bending the clutch-activating arm at a 90 degree angle. The front wheels also underwent alteration. Firestone cast centred wheels replaced the Dunlop wheels, and full solid cast wheels became optional as a balance weight, especially where a heavy duty winch had been fitted. In the

same period, the brass bushed front axle bearings were replaced with a taper roller bearing. This was a much-welcomed improvement and modification kits were produced for earlier models.

During 1941 there was a change in the casting of the cylinder head. The new head's decompression valve was situated at the front of the cylinder head as opposed to the side. Another change came about in 1943. As an attempt to gain greater horsepower output, a high compression head was made available and those tractors fitted with it reverted back to the side-mounted decompression valve. The reason for this is not very clear but it is assumed that it was to avoid waste of the former casting pattern, so as not to disrupt production of the cylinder heads in use at

A 1944 Marshall model M tractor fitted with driver's canopy, shown in the Yorkshire countryside
(B Laycock)

Production assembly line for model M at Britannia Works, Gainsborough 1944

the time. Another area to come under the Marshall spotlight was the strength of the castings. Problems with weakness in the rear axle casing of the former 12/20 were still very much in mind and fractures were still appearing in tractors fitted with winches when used to their limit. Eager to prevent a similar situation occurring, Marshalls took the precaution of giving the casting more strengthening webs and braces.

The colour scheme of the model M was very much the same as the 12/20, finished in green with silver wheel centres and decor. Occasionally Marshalls would paint the wheel centres red but always returned to silver. There was no particular reason for such a radical change in colour. Perhaps it was the frequent shortage of silver paint that motivated the change but rumour has it that it was all down to Marshalls' indecisiveness. By late 1940 it would appear that the colour scheme was finally decided upon, as from this date the wheel centres were painted red until the demise of the model M in June 1945.

Unfortunately, due to the loss of records, there is no official documentation relating to the full history of the model M. Production was very slow in the early years but with the passing of time, facilities and supplies improved and an examination of the serial numbers of those model Ms in preservation shows that eventually a flow was achieved against all odds. Production of the model M had commenced at serial no. 810 and ceased in June 1945 at somewhere between 1690 and 1700. Since Marshalls had discontinued their policy of jumping serial numbers by three, all the

Comparison view of the prototype Field Marshall Mark II contractors tractor and the 1944 model M (note the wartime front light fitted above the cylinder head on the model M)   (A Halstead)

model Ms produced followed consecutively. It is easy to figure that a total number of 890 were made between September 1938 and June 1945, allowing for the uncertainty over the last few.

As merchant shipping was a prime target for German U-boats during the war, overseas orders were suspended, with a few notable exceptions. Home orders were under Government control, which meant that nearly all the model Ms remained in Britain and Ireland.

Marshalls had long adopted a policy to continually strive to improve and modify their machines. It was no surprise that by 1943, when the model M was at its finest, the development team were already hard at work looking at ways in which to build on this tractor and its predecessor the 12/20. By 1944, a new Marshall tractor was undergoing field testing. Confident of a warm reception by the farming public and of high demand, Marshalls erected a new assembly track in the tractor shop at Britannia Works. On this new flow production line, the Field Marshall began life.

FIELD·MARSHALL

This is our new trade mark. Our well-known Britannia in a modern setting. You will not actually see the new name and symbol on our tractors until after the war. But it is the first evidence of the post-war plans we are making. There will be new "Field-Marshalls" to help you with a job as important in peace as in war.

We shall be glad to answer enquiries. Write to Department E.1.

MARSHALLS
OF GAINSBOROUGH
Tractors and Agricultural Machinery

Publicity advert announcing the new name Field Marshall November 1943

Nearly 1 Acre per Hour on 1 Gallon of Fuel

Recent tests have shown that you can run a Marshall Diesel Tractor for about 1/6th the cost of a petrol driven tractor.

On heavy ploughing, for instance, the Marshall tractor will use about 1 gallon of fuel per hour, while on light land the fuel

consumption is well under the gallon. The tests showed that for a full 8 hours' road hauling the tractor used only 5 gallons of fuel altogether.

Coupled with economy go great strength and durability—the Marshall tractor will haul a trailer weighing 9 tons up an incline of 1 in 6 without wheel slip.

1 **LOW LUBRICATING OIL CONSUMPTION.**
The lubricating oil consumption remains constant throughout the long life of the tractor. A unique system of lubrication measures out to each point the exact amount of oil required. This system of lubrication *does not allow increased consumption with wear.*

2 **SIXTY-SIX PARTS.**
The Marshall diesel tractor can claim to be the only tractor which has only 66 working and wearing parts. This simplicity of design and absence of unnecessarily delicate parts makes the Marshall tractor strong and long lasting, even under the most arduous conditions.

3 **CYLINDER WEAR.**
Tests show that it takes about 5-6 years' really heavy work to make a Marshall tractor show signs of cylinder wear. Then it is both cheap and simple to fit a new block.

4 **DECARBONISING.**
The Marshall diesel tractor can be decarbonised by *unskilled labour* in 3 hours. This operation is only necessary at most twice in a full year's working.

FIELD·MARSHALL

Marshall 12/20, fitted with a light duty winch
(B Poole)

Typical working environment for a Marshall model M with heavy duty winch and heavy cast front wheel weighted centres
(D Parker)

A 1941 Marshall model M complete with heavy duty winch
(B Tidbury)

Marshall single-cylinder RC20 8 ton road roller

Marshall T20 stationary power unit
(J Kick)

A late model M complete with lighting set

CHAPTER 5
A New Household Name in Farming, the Field Marshall

MARK I

The release of the Field Marshall, in June 1945, was the end-product of almost two years of intense research and practical testing. Although the new machine retained many of the characteristics of the model M, it was nevertheless a totally new tractor. It had a new shape, with stylish tinwork, influenced by the streamlined look of the American farm tractors that had been imported in large numbers under the lend-lease agreement. The name Field Marshall was part of a marketing strategy to create stronger product identification. Wanting to capitalise on their excellent reputation, it made sound business sense to give the firm's name a higher profile on all its products. Road rollers became Road Marshalls, threshing machines and combine harvesters Grain Marshalls, stationary steam engines and boilers Steam Marshalls. A new aluminium badge depicting a hand carrying a torch, with the Britannia crest at the top, was chosen as an emblem to be fitted to both tractors and rollers and assisted in the drive to create stronger product identification.

In January 1943 the design engineers had already began to visualise a new breed of tractor, and used a number of model M parts. A Field Marshall mock-up was constructed in the pattern shop at Britannia Works, with the new style bodywork made of wood to help picture the tractor's appearance. Marshalls initially intended to build three prototypes but due to the continual demand for arms artillery, the project was given low priority and work was restricted. By 1944, the erecting trestles were prepared to receive the casting that formed the main structure. A totally new construction, it resembled greatly the model M,

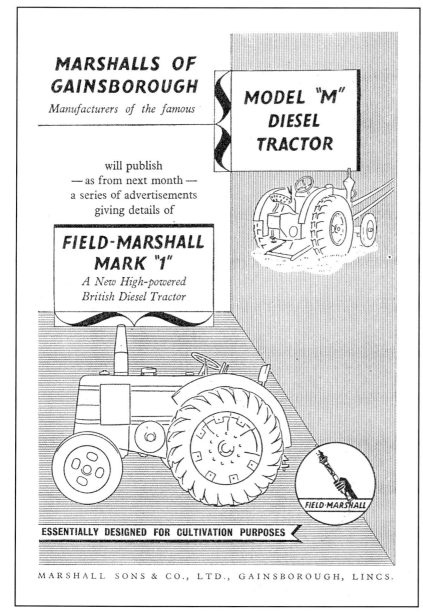

MARSHALLS OF GAINSBOROUGH
Manufacturers of the famous

MODEL "M" DIESEL TRACTOR

will publish
— as from next month —
a series of advertisements
giving details of

FIELD-MARSHALL MARK "1"
A New High-powered British Diesel Tractor

FIELD·MARSHALL

ESSENTIALLY DESIGNED FOR CULTIVATION PURPOSES

MARSHALL SONS & CO., LTD., GAINSBOROUGH, LINCS.

Announcing the release of the Field Marshall Mark I June 1945

MARSHALLS OF
GAINSBOROUGH

FIELD·MARSHALL

FIELD·MARSHALL
MARK "1"
*A New High-powered
British Diesel Tractor*

Field Marshall Mark I

with its gearbox and crankcase as one casting.

With a willing team of skilled and experienced engineers, the first Field Marshall was soon ready to undergo the usual field trials. Finished in buff primer, the machine sailed effortlessly through its tests without any major setbacks. The lengthy period during which it had been in development had certainly paid off. The tractor was then despatched to the National Institute of Agricultural Engineering (NIAE), at Silsoe, in Bedfordshire, in November, where it once again was able to proudly display its capabilities. After the first prototype had completed its run of tests, it was returned to Britannia Works where it was inspected, cleaned, sprayed and made ready for its starring role in the press release.

On the strength of its success, Marshalls proceeded to build two more prototype tractors followed by another 12 on the new production line. These production tractors were distributed to Marshalls' most loyal customers, in order to obtain some valuable feedback and eliminate any problems in the design. These machines received

serial numbers commencing with tractor no. 2001. As with the model M, Marshalls did not jump the numbers by three and followed on consecutively.

Since the Field Marshall had been built with the customer's requirements in mind, many of the model M's most impressive aspects had been further improved upon. The engine output was increased to 38 h.p. This was effected by simply uprating the fuel injection pressures and increasing the engine speed from 700 to 750 r.p.m. The bore and stroke remained the same as the model M and the 12/20. With this extra power the Field Marshall Mark I was very versatile, suitable for heavy cultivation and deep ploughing. It was able to haul a 4-furrow plough in average conditions and a 3-furrow plough in heavier ones. To help maintain traction, with the increased performance, the differential locking device became a standard feature. This could easily be applied when wheel slip occurred by depressing a lever conveniently positioned in front of the driver's seat. A completely new

Prototype Field Marshall Mark I tractor undergoing field test work at Warton, Gainsborough 1944

Prototype Field Marshall Mark I hauling Ransomes 3-furrow plough (note the absence of cartridge start)

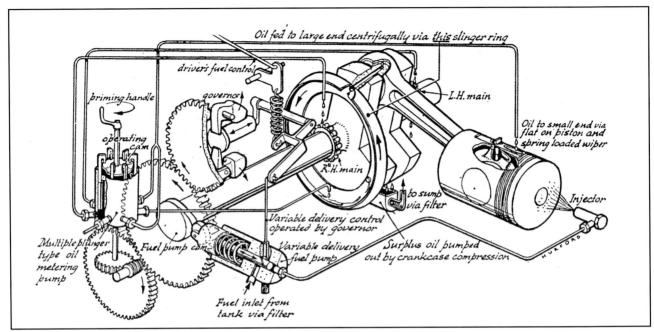

Fuel and oil system of Marshall single-cylinder engine

Rear view of prototype Mark I (note the screw-operated hand clutch wheel beneath the driver's seat)

driving arrangement with the seat and controls mounted on a platform, attached to the rear of the transmission housing, greatly increased the driver's visibility at the same time as bringing the foot and hand controls closer. To improve upon the cooling efficiency of the engine the cooling capacity was increased, by extending the header tank beyond the cylinder head. This expanded the cooling water capacity to 11 gallons from the model M's 9. It also provided a convenient securing point for the stylish front bonnet surround. In addition, the fuel tank saw an increase in size, which prolonged working periods before refuelling.

Along with the new styled tinwork, the Field Marshall Mark I featured a new cigar-shaped silencer. Except for those on the prototype tractors, these silencers were produced by Burgess of Hinckley in Leicestershire. The move to use outside suppliers was brought about in an attempt to reduce the workload on the already stretched workforce at Britannia Works. Edward Burgess was the Managing Director of Marshalls

at that time and was none other than the brother of the founder of the Burgess company. A spot of nepotism was the reason why Burgess continued to produce silencers throughout the full production of the Field Marshall range. In later years they continued to supply the MP6 and Track Marshall, as well as other leading tractor manufacturers like Fordson, Nuffield, Massey Harris, Ferguson and David Brown.

The transmission on the Mark I saw little change from that of the model M, with the exception that most of the gears and shafts were increased in diameter to provide more strength from the increase in power from the engine. The gear range still offered three forward speeds and a single reverse, varying from a bottom gear as low as 1.8 m.p.h. to a maximum speed of 6 m.p.h. in top gear. An optional high speed road gear of 9 m.p.h. was available but unlike the model M and 12/20 tractors, no other optional variations in range speeds were offered.

Perhaps Marshalls were a little too hasty when designing a new steering box for the Field

Rear view of the mock-up Mark I Field Marshall. Close inspection of the fuel tank and rear platform reveals that they are made of wood
(D Palmer)

Prototype Mark I prepared for publicity photo at Trent Works in 1945

Marshall. It was obvious that the one used on the 12/20 and model M was inappropriate, as it looked as though it was designed for a heavy commercial vehicle rather than for a 20 h.p. tractor. A reduction in its size would reduce materials and cost, but unfortunately the design team produced a steering box too small for the job. The steering on the Mark I was fairly light and the front wheels were cambered to reduce the amount of tyre drag and provide a sharper lock. In service the steering box on the Mark I and even on the later series 2 proved to be totally inadequate and failed constantly.

The first 12 Mark I tractors received the same wheels as fitted to the model M, with cast centres made by Firestone but with the name Marshalls cast into the outside face as a result of a gentleman's agreement. After tractor no. 2012, the front wheels were altered and became bolted to the hub by a series of five studs and nuts. These replaced the former system whereby the wheel could only be removed by totally stripping the front hub, as a result of which dirt and impurities would be introduced into the bearings. At the same time, the rear wheel centres also received a change in the casting pattern, with the omission of the cast blocks that were situated around the outside face of the wheel centre on previous models. By January 1946 the use of cast front and rear centres had been discontinued. Tractors around serial no. 2225 began to receive a new press steeled centre wheel made by G K N Sankey of Birmingham. The Sankey wheels helped considerably to reduce the weight of the machine; they were also much cheaper to buy and boosted Marshalls' profit margins. The reduction in weight of the tractor obviously reduced the ground pressure contact, lessening the chances of the machine becoming bogged down in soft ground. This reduction also had its

Rear view of prototype pre-production Field Marshall Mark I, Trent Works 1945

disadvantages, as reduction in weight on the rear drive axle would often result in the tractors inability to gain grip, and wheel spin would result. This problem was so widespread that service bulletins were issued to distributors, advising their customers to water ballast the rear wheels if this situation frequently occurred.

Like a number of 12/20s and early model M tractors, the Field Marshall wheel centres were painted silver. The bodywork green was darkened slightly to mid Brunswick green for the finishing coat.

Many of the minor changes in the Field Marshall's appearance were due to the difficulties with materials supply. The war had only just ended and materials were still very much in short supply, so where feasible Marshalls either adapted or simply omitted the parts providing they were not vital to the finished product. This accounts for several variations in the earlier models. One area that met with constant cutbacks was the panelwork. Often tractors did not receive all the strengthening braces to

support the rear wings, and the beading round the outer face of the wing would occasionally be omitted. Also the use of a lighter gauge material for the front and centre cowlings was not an uncommon practice.

Generally, the problems of the post-war years created difficulties in trying to fulfil the orders that were coming in for the Field Marshall. The factory had been geared up to arms production and Marshalls had to effect a major restructuring programme if they were to keep on top of the demand for their new tractor. Quite apart from the lack of stock, the war had depleted the workforce and so new workers had to be recruited. Such disruption obviously affected production levels, and in some instances customers faced a waiting list of up to six months. Despite constant apologies in the farming press to placate impatient clients, many farmers, understandably eager to re-equip their smallholdings after the war, cancelled their orders and gave their business to rival manufacturers. To forewarn future customers

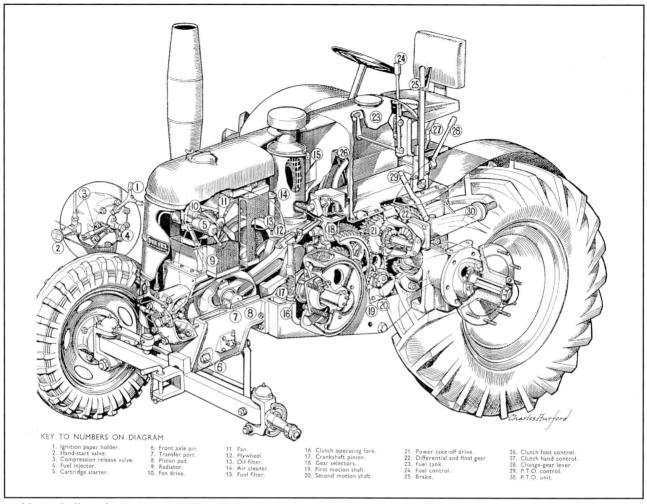

KEY TO NUMBERS ON DIAGRAM

1. Ignition paper holder.
2. Hand-start valve.
3. Compression release valve.
4. Fuel injector.
5. Cartridge starter.
6. Front axle pin.
7. Transfer port.
8. Piston pad.
9. Radiator.
10. Fan drive.
11. Fan.
12. Flywheel.
13. Oil filter.
14. Air cleaner.
15. Fuel filter.
16. Clutch operating fork.
17. Crankshaft pinion.
18. Gear selectors.
19. First motion shaft.
20. Second motion shaft.
21. Power take-off drive.
22. Differential and final gear.
23. Fuel tank.
24. Fuel control.
25. Brake.
26. Clutch foot control.
27. Clutch hand control.
28. Change-gear lever.
29. P.T.O. control.
30. P.T.O. unit.

Field Marshall Mark I

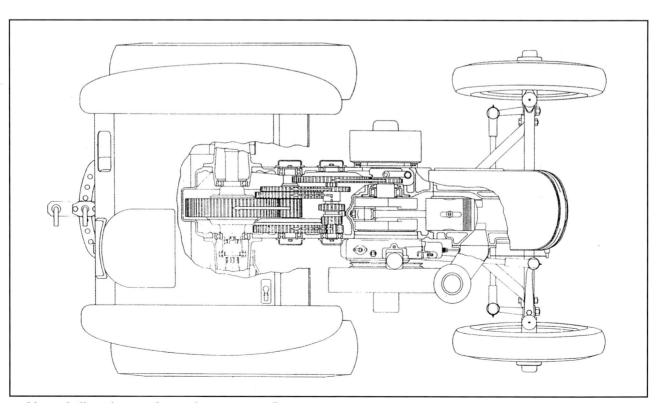

Field Marshall Mark I aerial view showing power flow arrangement

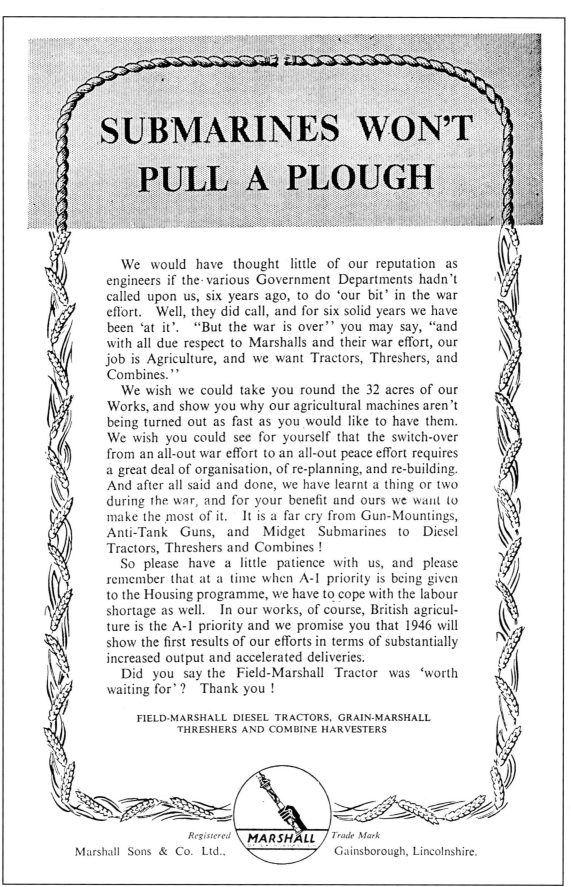

SUBMARINES WON'T PULL A PLOUGH

We would have thought little of our reputation as engineers if the various Government Departments hadn't called upon us, six years ago, to do 'our bit' in the war effort. Well, they did call, and for six solid years we have been 'at it'. "But the war is over" you may say, "and with all due respect to Marshalls and their war effort, our job is Agriculture, and we want Tractors, Threshers, and Combines."

We wish we could take you round the 32 acres of our Works, and show you why our agricultural machines aren't being turned out as fast as you would like to have them. We wish you could see for yourself that the switch-over from an all-out war effort to an all-out peace effort requires a great deal of organisation, of re-planning, and re-building. And after all said and done, we have learnt a thing or two during the war, and for your benefit and ours we want to make the most of it. It is a far cry from Gun-Mountings, Anti-Tank Guns, and Midget Submarines to Diesel Tractors, Threshers and Combines !

So please have a little patience with us, and please remember that at a time when A-1 priority is being given to the Housing programme, we have to cope with the labour shortage as well. In our works, of course, British agriculture is the A-1 priority and we promise you that 1946 will show the first results of our efforts in terms of substantially increased output and accelerated deliveries.

Did you say the Field-Marshall Tractor was 'worth waiting for' ? Thank you !

FIELD-MARSHALL DIESEL TRACTORS, GRAIN-MARSHALL
THRESHERS AND COMBINE HARVESTERS

Registered **MARSHALL** *Trade Mark*

Marshall Sons & Co. Ltd., Gainsborough, Lincolnshire.

Explanation for delays in production of the Field Marshall Mark I, December 1945

about the delay, Marshalls began to include in their sales literature a mention that it would be prudent to order a Field Marshall well before it was needed.

Until the mid 1930s the normal method of starting an engine was by starting handle. As time progressed the motor car had developed further and the use of the electric starter was gradually passed down to the farm tractor. By 1935 most of the world's leading manufacturers had an electric starting option available on their machines. Whilst sales for Marshall tractors had not been greatly threatened by the existence of electric start tractors, nevertheless there was an increasing demand for Marshalls to offer an alternative starting device. The general feedback from customers, especially the older ones, was that the Marshall was not a particularly easy machine to greet on a cold winter morning. Even though it was an easy engine to start once over compression, the degree of physical exertion required in order to achieve this stage was annoying. Since the Marshall engine was not the conventional multi-cylinder type, it was necessary to look at alternative starting devices, as the electric start was out of the question. A starter motor and the number of batteries required to turn the engine over would have necessitated a radical change in the structure of the tractor, making the incorporation of electric starting a prohibitively expensive exercise. It was more cost effective for Marshalls to investigate other methods, including petrol starting, compressed air starting and a small donkey engine. All of these ideas mooted were too complicated and thus uneconomical.

Finally, inspiration came when Marshall engineers ventured into the aeronautical world and researched the use of a power start cartridge device. At last there was a fairly simple and fail-safe way of starting an engine. All that was involved was to put a charged explosion in front of the piston when the engine was on top dead centre. The force of the explosion would send the piston backwards, revolving the crankshaft at such speed that it would initiate combustion, thus bringing the engine into life. A simple cartridge filled with carbon pellets provided this source of power and was easily adapted to the Marshall engine because of its own simple construction. All that was required was a

modification to the cylinder head, to allow the charge to enter the combustion chamber via the decompression valve and a shut-off valve for when reverting back to hand start. Initially, the provision of a cartridge that was capable of starting the Marshall engine caused a number of problems and most of the developmental work was trial and error. At the cost of a number of cylinder heads, blocks and crankshafts, the ideal formulation was found.

The starting procedure involved inserting a cartridge into a special breach beneath the header tank on the left-hand side of the tractor. A simple screw thread secured the breach cap and incorporated a detonation pin. After the tractor had been prepared for starting, all that was required was a gentle tap of the firing pin which would immediately make the engine burst into life. As these cartridges were of the same size and dimensions as those for an ordinary shotgun, Marshalls embossed their crest on them so as to prevent any confusion. However, rumour abounded amongst the farming community that it was possible to use ordinary cartridges. Marshalls tried to dispel such talk by carrying out an experiment. A tractor was set up and tried using an ordinary shotgun cartridge but with the fuel level shut off the engine failed to rotate even half a turn. When the Marshall cartridge was applied, the flywheel spun round no less than seven times. This put paid to any further improvisation attempts.

Due to setbacks in its development, the cartridge start was not ready for the release of the first Field Marshalls. Marshalls were also a little sceptical about the appeal of this power starting device and accordingly chose to omit it from their sales literature and press releases. The first 12 were thus sold without it but were returned later to receive this modification. Despite Marshalls' pessimism, the cartridge start met with overwhelming success, with some customers requesting that their 12/20s and model Ms received the conversion. Once in service, the cartridge start did have its shortcomings. It was believed that its continuous use and the sudden shock from the explosions could cause premature little end failure. Another problem which came to light was with the decompression valve getting jammed, due to the deposits of granules from the cartridge which would often

Cartridge starting

Production Mark I Field Marshall hauling a Grain Marshall 568 combine harvester in 1946
(A Halstead)

Model M and Field Marshall Mark II contractors tractor at Trent Works, Gainsborough in 1944. Trent Works was situated roughly a mile away from Britannia Works and was used as a test bed area and paint shop for the single-cylinder tractors commencing the later part of the Second World War
(A Halstead)

require re-seating or even renewal. Generally, however, the move to a more user-friendly starting method was extremely successful.

During the initial development stages of the Field Marshall, Marshalls realised that there was a need to provide the same optional facilities that were popular with the model M. The feature in most constant demand was the winch. Although both heavy and light duty winches were adequate and relatively trouble free, Marshalls decided to design one single unit that could be used for both heavy and light applications. The Field Marshall Mark II was the end result. At last here was a tractor strictly designed for the job, not adapted for it, and one that was particularly geared towards their most popular customer, the threshing contractor. The Field Marshall Mark II, or the contractors tractor as it became known, was developed alongside the standard Mark I. The Mark II was certainly among the first 12 Field Marshalls produced without the cartridge start.

The Mark II's standard features included a full CAV lighting set, canvas-framed canopy and a 9 m.p.h. top speed gear, but it was the winch that made this model so popular. Whereas the model M fitted with a heavy duty winch had been a rather uncomfortable machine to operate, in the Mark II all operations of the winch, except for

lowering the anchors, could be accomplished from the driving seat. Obviously a great deal of thought had gone into the layout and construction of this tractor, with the winch drum and drive assembly being neatly tucked away beneath the driver's platform.

Another selling point was that operation of the Field Marshall was relatively simple. The drum was driven by a duplex roller chain which took its drive from a special power take-off gearbox driven from the first motion shaft of the tractor's gearbox. The power take-off gearbox incorporated a dog clutch and could be engaged and disengaged by a single lever in hand's reach of the driving seat, after disengaging the engine clutch. The sprocket brake drum was keyed into a pinion shaft that meshed with an internal gear onto the roped drum. The winch brake was similar to the tractor's rear wheel drum brakes with the operating lever conveniently placed, also reachable from the driver's seat. When the lever was applied it operated upon a cam that in turn locked the Ferodo-lined shoes on the inner face of the drum, which provided a suitable brake and allowed the driver to operate the machine in the normal manner without uncoupling the rope. The winch drum had a capacity of 75 yd of $5/8$ in diameter wire rope exerting a mean line pull at the drum of 8500 lb. The rope speed was varied by the position of the engine throttle lever giving a variation of speeds between 64 and 120 ft per minute. The anchors were of robust channel iron construction and were easily lowered into their working position. When not in use the anchors could be lifted into their travel position and latched, thus providing ideal security in rough terrain.

As the Mark II was purpose-built for use by contractors, Marshalls took into account the amount of load the machine would need to haul and consequently the effort required to stop the tractor. The braking system on the basic farm tractor had proved to be rather inadequate and several complaints were raised by farmers operating threshing outfits in the Highlands and other mountainous areas. To help combat the problem of overrunning, the Mark II was fitted with additional hind wheel drum brakes along with the standard transmission brake. This provided additional stopping power but gave the control area a rather confused collection of brake levers.

To enable contractors to move their outfit in the dark, a CAV 12 volt dynamo lighting system was provided, consisting of a single 60 watt headlamp positioned in front of the exhaust pipe, two 6 watt side lamps fitted to the front of each rear wheel fender and a single tail lamp fitted beside the rear number plate. An optional 36 watt rear spotlight was also available.

The full canvas canopy, designed with the contractor's need to work in all types of weather, provided both shelter and shade. Its construction left much to be desired and often a low branch was all that was needed to cause its decapitation.

To compensate for the additional weight of the winch over the rear axle, the Mark II was provided with a pair of front end weights. They were specifically designed to be mounted above and around the cylinder head and were disguised by the front engine cowling. Optional extras included an extension for the exhaust pipe called a threshing top; this became standard equipment on tractors produced after June 1946. Optional choices of 12¼ in x 28 in rear tyres and a driver's rear view mirror were also available. The front push pole bracket, which was essential for setting up the threshing outfit in confined spaces, became standard in both Mark I and Mark II

Rear view of Field Marshall winch

The result of poor judgement when coming to the end of the furrow. This Mark I Field Marshall disappeared into a dike and broke in half
(S Archer)

A literally exploded view of the stricken Field Marshall on page 77, clearly showing the piston and crankshaft
(S Archer)

Typical scene of the 1940s. Field Marshall Mark I tractor pulls alongside a straw rick with Marshall threshing drum
(O Mitchell)

tractors. Whilst the Mark I had a standard 6 m.p.h. with the option of 9 m.p.h., the Mark II offered a standard top speed of 9 m.p.h. with the option of the slower 6 m.p.h. and accommodated the needs of those contractors working in hilly areas.

The Mark II was fairly expensive in comparison with its competitors, but it offered all these additions as standard equipment. In 1945 its

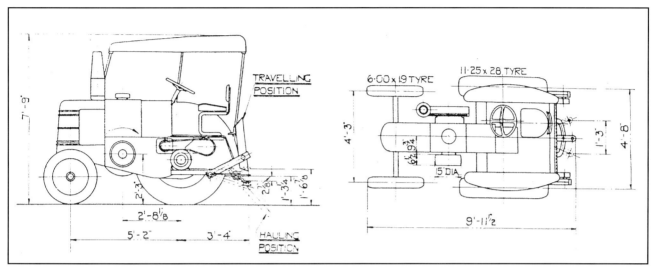

Overall dimensions for Field Marshall Mark II contractors tractor

Gainsborough in flood in 1947. Marshalls loaned brand new tractors to the stricken town to aid with the rescue of stranded families (S Archer)

The oldest surviving Field Marshall, second production tractor no. 2. Fitted with model M cast wheels

Field Marshall Mark I no. 6, restored to its former condition without the facility of cartridge starting

Field Marshall Mark I with later style cast wheel centres

Late example of a 1947 Field Marshall Mark I

price was just in excess of £840, with the standard Mark I being £550. Due to the vast price discrepancy, many farmers considered it more expedient to buy the standard Mark I and adapt the winch from their old tractor to fit. There are many examples to be seen today of this somewhat ad hoc attempt at DIY, with Mark I tractors fitted with model M winches and those of other manufacturers such as Hesford, Lainchbury and Boughton.

Field Marshall Mark II contractors tractor, complete with rag-top canopy

SERIES 2

Although the Mark I was undoubtedly a resounding success, Marshalls did not rest on their laurels but immediately began thinking about its successor, as competition was rife. Apart from the continual presence of imported American tractors, several new British companies had surfaced. With the economy increasingly geared to reviving farm produce output, there obviously followed a tractor boom. The Morris Motor Company from Oxford were in the process of launching their Nuffield range of tractors, whilst Vivian Loyd & Company Ltd from Camberley had commenced making crawlers by using Brenn gun carrier tracks. Farm mechanisation had been greatly influenced by the introduction of the 3-point linkage system

designed by Harry Ferguson, for this led to other manufacturers emulating this. The Ford Motor Company from Dagenham had produced the E27N Major, which became one of Marshalls' strongest rivals. Due to Ford's ability to mass produce, tractors could be supplied on demand and at half the cost. Most of Marshalls' rivals were still providing petrol/paraffin engine tractors, since the use of the diesel engine was still uncommon. The Field Marshall maintained its advantage, as its simplicity and reputation for being economical to run helped ward off the competition.

During the two years that the Mark I was in production, Marshalls kept their ear to the ground and listened to the feedback from their customers. The Field Marshall series 2, introduced

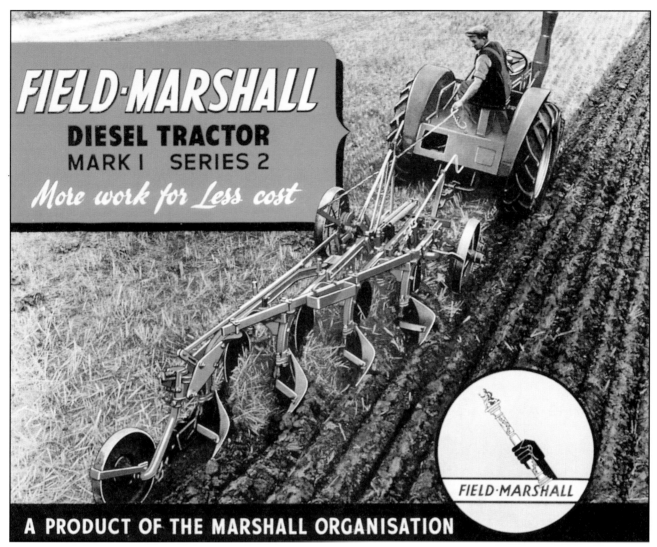

Field Marshall Mark I series 2

Field Marshall series 2 making its first public appearance at the Royal Show, Lincoln, in July 1947

Publicity announcement for the release of the Field Marshall series 2, September 1947

in July 1947, and on the market in September, was the result. This new machine incorporated many of the improvements suggested by their loyal clientele. Marshalls took out advertisement space in the farming press and covered the eight main improvements to the specification:

1. Increased power from 38 to 40 h.p.
2. Improved bearings.
3. Improved brakes.
4. Better engine cooling.
5. Larger clutch for smoother operation.
6. More comfortable driving seat.
7. Independent brakes.
8. Increased rear tyre section for improved adhesion.

The increase in power from 38 to 40 h.p. was very much welcomed. There had been several complaints about the Mark I, with customers disputing its working capabilities. It was not so much that the tractor could not reach its maximum performance; it was more a question of being able to maintain it. The increase in large farm implements such as 4-furrow ploughs began to necessitate a greater horsepower output. The increase was achieved in the series 2 not by increasing the r.p.m., which would have been the simple option, but by modifying the cylinder block, enlarging the induction ports, swirl chamber and changing the spray formation of the vaporiser plate to displace a wider and finer jet over the piston's face. The fuel injection pump was also uprated but still maintained the same delivery pressure of 2000 lb. It is interesting to note that Marshalls achieved the increase to 40 h.p., which was double that of the 12/20, without increasing the size of the cylinder bore. The basic

A 1947 Field Marshall series 2 Mark I (standard agricultural) tractor

Rear view of standard agricultural model series 2

character of the engine remained the same as with the 12/20 and had a 6½ in bore and 9 in stroke.

The series 2 featured the new needle roller little end bearing that had proved to be more successful than the troublesome bronzed bush used previously. The crankshaft main roller bearing on the governor housing side of the tractor also saw improvement and was replaced by a ball race bearing. This bearing became problematic and was discontinued in tractors produced after October 1948, when Marshalls reverted back to the taper roller bearing previously used on the Mark I.

The 6-bladed cooling fan previously used in the Mark I had not been entirely satisfactory. Marshalls overcame this by simply reverting to the 4-blade fan that had been used in the model M

tractor, with only a slight increase in the fan blade section to produce a greater flow of air. It was a rather simple move but enough to warrant a mention in the advertising literature. To allow for smoother operation and to eliminate the fierce snatching of the clutch, the cone and outer face of the clutch were increased in diameter by 2 in and the angle of the cone was reduced. The increase in the outer face would obviously increase the speed of the belt and hence required more power from the tractor. Certainly it reduced the tractor's performance whenever it was used to power belt-driven machinery, such as a saw bench. Marshalls had taken this into account and compensated for the extra effort needed with the new high powered engine, although some farmers who maintained a large selection of Marshall tractors argued that a Mark I and even a model M would outperform a

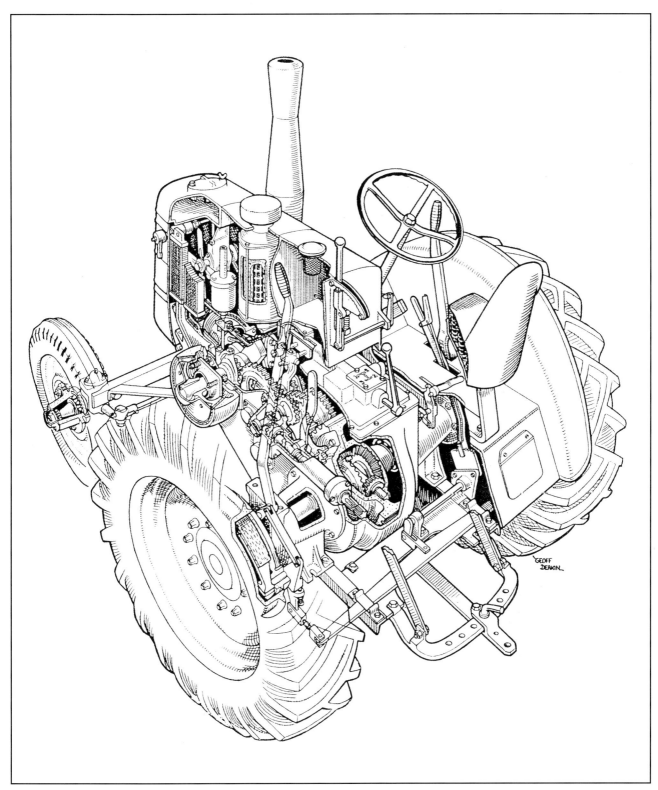

Field Marshall series 2

series 2 on belt work.

The gearbox layout remained basically unchanged. There were a small number of alterations incorporated into the new tractor, one of which was the omission of the transmission parking brake. By increasing the size of the drum and shoes of the rear brakes, ample stopping power was provided, as well as an efficient and reliable parking brake. This allowed Marshalls to discontinue the former braking system, where the

Mark II series 2 contractors tractor standing in front of the massive grain silos at Trent Works, Gainsborough 1948

A 1948 Field Marshall Mark II series 2 contractors tractor hauling a Marshall S. M. steel framed threshing machine and Jones high density baler

Series 2 production line, Britannia Works 1948

brake was incorporated into the first speed gear on the second motion shaft. It had been an efficient braking system in so far as it brought the machine to a halt but had proved to be slightly troublesome whenever the brake needed to be relined, as access was difficult and entailed virtually stripping down the gearbox. The clutch pedal transmission brake remained unchanged and when adjusted easily provided another way of stopping the tractor, preferably without a load. Although the series 2 brakes were undoubtedly a great improvement to those on the Mark I, brake failure as the machines aged, usually due to worn oil seals and brake linings, was not unheard of.

Two levers situated either side of the driver's seat enabled the operator to move each hind wheel brake independently and also assisted the steering whenever a sharp turn was needed. Indeed it allowed the tractor to be turned around within its own length. The independent brake was also very effective in controlling the differential whenever wheel spin occurred, since the operator

could simply transmit the drive to the opposite wheel. Marshalls were confident that this simple and effective way of regaining traction did not warrant the use of the differential lock that had been previously used on the Mark I. They were quite happy that the new system provided the means of overcoming wheel slip without putting the transmission through any unwanted stress. This system was obviously not as efficient as the mechanical locking device, since applying the brakes reduced the engine's performance, which needed to be top class when hauling a 4-furrow plough.

It is rumoured that the differential lock was discontinued for a number of other reasons, one of which was misuse. If the driver forgot that the lever had been applied, he lost control of the steering. Another reason was the tractor's excessive torque in the lower speed range, which caused damage to the transmission and rear axle castings.

The differential lock was not alone in causing problems with damaged axle castings. Tractors

Field Marshall Mark II series 2 contractors tractor

fitted with winches also suffered, especially if the tractor was regularly put under heavy loads beyond the capabilities of both tractor and winch. Due to the fractures that appeared in the Mark I transmission casings, the series 2 received extra strengthening braces within its structure. The rear axle, half shaft and hub were redesigned and strengthened to accommodate the extra horsepower delivered from the engine. It should be noted that this is one area where the Mark I and series 2 can be easily identified, as by simply looking at the centre hub of the rear wheel it is possible to tell them apart. If the hub is noticeably raised with a cap it is a Mark I or Mark II but if the hub is flush with the wheel centre then it is a series 2. The series 2 has a flatter hub face with two $^3/_4$ in Whitworth hexagon headed bolts positioned diagonally opposite each other, which serve to keep the

View from rear, showing winch in working position

Marshalls celebrating their centenary year at the 1948 Royal Show, York

hub-extracting threads in good order when overhauling the brakes. It would appear that problems still occurred with fracturing around the rear axle castings, as service bulletins refer to another change in the castings on machines produced after January 1949.

The optional 12³⁄₄ in x 18 in rear tyres available on the Mark I became a standard feature of the series 2. The tyre size was again increased after the first batch of 350 tractors, to 13 in x 28 in. The series 2 still suffered from a lack of traction and Marshalls repeated the issuing of a series of service bulletins to their distributors, in which it was explained how to water ballast the rear wheels. The front tyre section still retained the same 600 in x 19 in tyre section but due to continual problems with the wheel rims splitting on the Mark I, especially if fitted with front end weights, the scalloped hole pattern was discontinued in favour of a plain rim to give extra support.

A new exhaust silencer was introduced, again supplied by Burgess. The design and shape helped to reduce the echo associated with the cigar-shaped silencers. The shape and tinwork on

the series 2 remained unchanged. As production and demand increased, several alterations came about when Marshalls let out work to outside contractors. During the early part of 1948, Sankey were contracted to produce the rear mudguards; these were a press formed unit and noticeably narrower than Marshall-made ones. The Sankey wings were gradually filtered onto the assembly line, thus leading to the erratic appearance of the earlier models. By mid 1948, after tractor no. 5400, the Marshall-made mudguards were discontinued and all tractors which left Britannia Works thereafter were fitted with the Sankey version. Other noticeable modifications during the production of the series 2 were changes in the gear lever and throttle casting. The flat tulip-shaped levers were superseded by a rounded knob which was more comfortable to handle. This revision gradually filtered through with tractors receiving one or the other before rounded gear levers and throttle knobs became uniform in mid 1948.

The contractors model of the series 2 was identified as the Mark II series 2. Standard models were known simply as the series 2 and

Six series 2 Field Marshall tractors belonging to distributors T H White, on display in Devizes, Wiltshire in 1948

A 1949 example of a Field Marshall Mark II series 2 contractors tractor complete with Portland cab

Field Marshall Mark II series 2 contractors tractor

there can often be a certain amount of confusion with the earlier Mark II contractors model. Fundamentally, the winch retained the same specification as the former contractors model and so remained virtually the same. The flimsy rag-top canopy was replaced by a glass-framed cab manufactured by Portland Engineering of Halifax in Yorkshire, though this was not a standard feature and simply remained optional. It did not prove to be a great success, as even though it provided shelter from the elements and protected the operator from the smuts emitted from the exhaust, it also absorbed every vibration. The noise was transmitted by the framework construction, acting as a makeshift antennae, resulting in one very deafened driver.

The series 2 contractors tractor still featured the CAV lighting equipment as previously, using a

12 volt dynamo to provide the power. For customers who did not require a heavy winch, a smaller one made by Hesford was available. This winch was particularly suitable for threshing contractors and general light winching duties. It was not as robust as the Marshall winch but much easier to operate due to the simplicity of its construction. The Hesford winch was driven by chain from a sprocket fixed to the tractor's power take-off shaft, whereupon a worm and wheel would supply the drive to the cone clutch that engaged the winch drum. The winch had a mean line pull of 10,000 lb on a bare drum and carried 60 ft of $\frac{1}{2}$ in diameter wire rope. Marshalls had an agreement with Hesford to promote this winch as an alternative to their own and also to incorporate a Marshall makers plate to the gearbox side cover. This particular winch suited most makes of

An impressive line-up of Field Marshall tractors belonging to Caroni Ltd of Trinidad

Stability problems were overcome with this tractor in New Zealand by fitting dual rear wheels

tractor and was known as the big minor tractor winch when supplied directly from Hesford.

By November 1947 Marshalls had production of the series 2 in full swing. All the problems with obtaining parts and materials that had affected the manufacture of the Mark I had been eliminated with plentiful supplies. Marshalls were able to enjoy increased production levels in the midst of a post-war boom. As acquiring parts and supplies was no longer an issue and more

importantly, the political barriers erected during the war were no longer in place, Marshalls took the opportunity to rekindle their business relationships with their overseas customers and brought about a large increase in export orders. Many of their tractors left the docks to find homes in France, Sweden, Switzerland, Africa, India, Canada, Australia, New Zealand, West Indies, Thailand, Spain, Italy and Ireland.

To illustrate the lushness of overseas trade at

this time, it can be noted that during the two years of production, Marshalls exported one-third of their series 2 tractors, with the largest orders coming from France, Australia, Africa and Canada. In general, most of the series 2s sold overseas were the standard agricultural tractor, and very few contractors models were ordered. Marshalls also found a niche in Third World countries where the Field Marshall's reputation for simple operation, low maintenance costs and exceptional fuel economy made it an ideal machine. In many of these countries the tractors were operated by native drivers with limited experience, and the need for cheapness and efficiency were important prerequisites.

Several alterations were made for the export market, mainly due to the difference in climate. An air intake extension was made available as an optional piece of equipment for those machines working in dusty environments but was discontinued in June 1948 and replaced by a Vokes pre-cleaner element. This subsequently became a standard fitting on all tractors working in warmer and dustier climates, due to a number of complaints received of poor engine performance and premature wear which was simply due to dust entering the combustion chamber. A colonial lighting set was also available for export models which had the

regular 12 volt dynamo system, the difference being that the single front headlamps were replaced by two headlamps mounted on each mudguard, in place of the sidelights. Spade lugg wheels were fitted to pre-empt the difficulty in obtaining replacement tyres in such far-flung corners of the world as the West Indies.

Towards the end of production of the series 2 several improvements to specification and build were made, prompted by customer feedback and filtered through both the home market and overseas to reach Marshalls' ears. Tractors working in the extreme heat and tough environments of the tropics were certainly put to

An impressive way of boosting the tractor's output. It was fairly common practice in Australia and New Zealand to join two tractors in tandem

The series 2 shunting tractor. Only two tractors of this kind were produced
(Rural History Centre, University of Reading)

Field Marshall series 2 with Roadless half track conversion, Fowlers feared that these half track conversions would jeopardise sales of their VF crawler; therefore, further development of them was discouraged. (V Dodge)

the test, as if any component was going to fail it would do so under these conditions. The series 2 was also subjected to extremely cold climates, with tractors exported to Norway performing in sub-zero temperatures. A recurrent problem that came to light with machines sent to work in such cold locations was that diesel would often freeze up in the fuel tanks. The tank was positioned so far away from the engine that it did not benefit from the heat produced, which would have kept the diesel at a warmer temperature. It was impossible to mount the fuel tank elsewhere, due to the tractor's construction. The problem was easily remedied by adding paraffin to the diesel. Paraffin having a much lower freezing point than diesel meant that the engine would run on part or full paraffin mixture. The machine did not run as efficiently as on diesel but at least it dealt with the problem.

Whilst any recurring faults would be dealt with by Marshalls' own service engineers, some problems entailed a major overhaul and revamp. The oily smuts of waste oil that were deposited from a 2-stroke diesel engine had always been an

issue and the Marshall engine was no exception. Several attempts to deal with the problem had been made, including changing the quality of the piston rings and re-calibrating the oil pump, but all of these were in vain. The fact remained that the Marshall engine emitted oil smuts, especially when the tractor was engaged in only light duties. As the exhaust pipe was positioned directly in front of the driver, it was inevitable that drivers would catch a share of oily deposits in their face. It was a standard joke in the farming community, with the drivers being ribbed about the change in their complexions. The problem was serious enough to warrant some farmers swapping allegiance from Marshalls to another tractor manufacturer. Far from combating the problem at source, Marshalls simply tried to reduce the amount of smuts by incorporating an oil catcher in the exhaust pipe to gather the oil in a trough. With a further waste oil pipe built into the silencer, the oil was deposited into the atmosphere. This system was not entirely effective but it reduced the deposits considerably, at least until the trough became blocked with carbon,

Early series 2 equipped with Roadless skeleton half tracks   (V Dodge)

when the problem reoccurred. In August 1949 Marshalls instructed Burgess to proceed with the new improved silencer, with tractors thereafter receiving the modified unit.

Burgess were not only involved with supplying silencers, as towards the end of the production life of the series 2 they were also contracted to supply an oil bath air filter pre-cleaner. This was shaped like a large mushroom and could be inserted into the existing filter housing without recourse to any major alterations. The benefit of a pre-cleaner was the reduction of impurities entering the main filter unit, as the dust particles were collected inside a trough built into the base of the pre-cleaner housing. It was particularly beneficial in cases where tractors were working in a dusty environment or indeed employed on threshing duties, for such conditions often necessitated that the main filter be cleaned out at least once a day. The addition of the Burgess pre-cleaner meant that the main filter would not

require attention for at least a week. Whilst it was standard equipment on all tractors produced after October 1949, because of its efficiency and popular demand, it became available as a separate item to fit all the previous models of Marshall single-cylinder tractors and cost £2 15s 0d.

Towards the end of production of the series 2, several additional improvements were made to the specification of the tractor. Those tractors built after serial no. 9000 witnessed the steady introduction of the new strengthened Sankey rear wheel centre. This new centre had a plain-faced inner dish and was gradually phased in as the old pattern rear wheel centre became obsolete. After serial no. 10500 all series 2 tractors had this new style of wheel.

Other notable improvements were made to enhance the quality of the tractor. The front cowling saw a slight alteration when its opening was enlarged, to achieve an easier access to the ignition pin. The use of Firestone 14 in x 28 in

For the information of

Marshall and Fowler Tractor Distributors, November, 1949

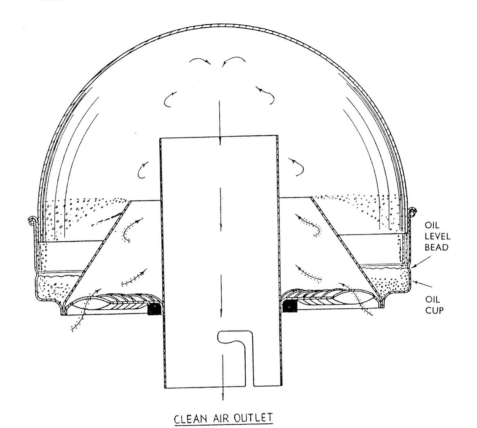

CLEAN AIR OUTLET

DIAGRAM KEY	
	DUSTY AIR
	CLEAN AIR
	DUST PARTICLES
	DUST LADEN OIL

The " Burgess " Centrifugal Oil Bath Air Cleaner
(Type OBC)

In collaboration with Burgess Products Co. Ltd., an improved primary air filter has been developed and can be simply and easily fitted to the Field Marshall Series I and II, and also to the Fowler Mark VF Diesel Crawler Tractor.

These air filters are available from Marshall Sons & Co. Ltd., and John Fowler & Co. (Leeds) Ltd.

This primary air filter shows a marked improvement in filtration efficiency over previous types, it is easy to clean and maintain and sets up a minimum of resistance to air flow under all conditions. It has been especially developed for exceptionally dusty conditions, but will also give improved performances in less arduous circumstances.

Introduction of the Burgess pre-cleaner for Field Marshall and Fowler VF crawler

An extremely late version of a Field Marshall series 2 on display at the Royal Smithfield Show, Earls Court, London in December 1949 (note the Burgess pre-cleaner and late wheel centres)

rear section tyres became available as an optional extra to enhance traction. The flywheel also received further machining to create a stepped groove around its outer face. This alteration was not in any way connected with improving the tractor's performance, as it was strictly a cost-cutting exercise. By allowing the tool that cut the decompression thread to have a firmer contact with the face, machining difficulties were overcome and so material wastage was reduced.

Production was finally discontinued in December 1949 to make way for a new improved tractor that had been in development since the summer of 1948. There is some mystery as to the total production number of the series 2 and this has long been a subject for dispute amongst enthusiasts. Commencing at serial no. 4025 in September 1947 and finishing at serial no. 11024 in December 1949 would account for one under

7000 units. Some quarters of the tractor preservation movement have said that Marshalls simply did not have the facilities to account for this huge total and that probably Marshalls had once again reverted to their favoured policy of jumping serial numbers to confuse rival manufacturers. Taking this argument on board, the question begs to be asked as to why Marshalls should feel a need to resort to such a tactic. The series 2 was produced at a post-war boom time when demand for these machines was often greater than supply. Another argument is that the model M, the Mark I and all the tractors produced after the series 2 are consecutive in number, so why should the series 2 not have followed suit?

Having consulted several ex-Marshall employees still living in the Gainsborough area, all of whom were directly involved on the factory floor, I have found that not one of them could recall Marshalls employing the policy of jumping

French distributors S.E.D.I.M. stand at the 1949 Paris Agricultural Show
(J Barbier)

Thirty-five Field Marshall series 2 tractors en route to Algiers   (R Walker)

Field Marshall series 2 being lowered into the hold of a ship destined for Sweden in 1949
(R Walker)

numbers during the Field Marshall series. However, an illuminating fact to emerge from my research was that Marshalls management apparently exerted a great deal of pressure on the workforce to produce a certain quota at the end of each calendar month, and the desired output was no less than 280 machines. All the stops were pulled out to ensure that these figures were achieved and indeed improved upon, which necessitated staff working overtime, through the night and well into the following day. Since the series 2 was produced over a period of 27 months and assuming the quota of 280 units per month was fulfilled, this would account for a total of 7560 tractors. Allowing for some deductions for initial pre-production difficulties and the reduction of output towards the end, it does make the suggested figure of nearly 7000

machines more convincing. Unfortunately there is no documentary evidence in existence to help shed some light on this matter, since all tractor records for this period were destroyed.

In conclusion, the fact that the series 2 outnumbers any other model by at least three to one on the rally fields of Britain even today must surely say something about its popularity and numbers. Although production ceased in December 1949, it was still available while stocks remained. Some were still being sold as late as June 1950, especially to overseas distributors in France, Australia and Canada. The Royal Smithfield Show at Earls Court, London, in December 1949 displayed two series 2 tractors on the Marshall Fowler stand. The new series 3 was not there, as it was still under development and had not been officially released.

Early 1947 Field Marshall series 2

A 1948 Field Marshall series 2 fitted with Sankey narrow rear wings

A 1947 Field Marshall Mark II series 2 contractors tractor, complete with Portland cab

Adrolic rear mounted 3-point linkage system fitted to a Field Marshall series 2 tractor

Field Marshall series 2 equipped with spade lugg wheels, an unusual and rare feature

A 1949 example of a Field Marshall series 2 complete with lights and later Sankey rear wheel centres

CHAPTER 6
From Tracks to Tyres

In 1946 Thos W Ward Ltd acquired a controlling interest in John Fowler & Company (Leeds) Ltd, a well-established firm that had been producing agricultural machinery since 1850. Marshall and Fowler had enjoyed a good business relationship over the past hundred years; they had remained rivals and had competed fiercely in the market for traction engine and road roller sales world-wide. It was Fowlers' excellence in producing steam ploughing tackle that had earned them their reputation, and much of their success thereafter was built on this. The declining fall in sales, due to the overall demise of steam power, meant that Fowlers had to try to compensate for the loss by introducing their own range of motor tractors. They chose to concentrate on the specialised crawler tractor market, which was dominated by the American Caterpillar. Their effort to emulate the success of the Caterpillar was not entirely satisfactory, especially during the early stages of production. The FD range introduced in 1944 had shown mild promise and increased popularity, particularly in the fen lands of Lincolnshire. Powered by a Freeman Sanders diesel engine, the FD tractor was made available in a range of 25 to 55 h.p.

Although Fowlers achieved moderate success within this specialised market, it had nevertheless done very little to compensate for the increasing lack of steam ploughing tackle sales, and they found themselves falling into a rapid financial decline. A takeover bid was inevitable and in a clever move Thos Ward married two of Britain's largest engineering companies, as Marshalls themselves had been associated with Thos Ward for ten years. Any further success with the FD series was blighted by the takeover, since sanctions were imposed upon the further use of the Freeman Sanders engine. Since the Field Marshall series 2 was met with overwhelming success, it was suggested that perhaps the Freeman Sanders engine could be replaced by the Field Marshall's single-cylinder engine. However, because of the unusual construction of the Marshall engine, it would have been difficult to adapt it to suit the FD3 crawler. Finally the decision was made to cease production of the FD3, much to the chagrin of Fowler employees who considered the move to a single-cylinder engine from a multi-cylinder a step backwards. There was an initial resentment amongst the ex-Fowler employees, who were witnessing their tractor being sent to the scrap heap as a result of the exorbitant costs involved in fitting a Marshall single-cylinder engine. These differences of opinion were soothed somewhat by the management's decision to develop a totally new tractor that would utilise the skills and expertise of both Marshall and Fowler, a product to celebrate the integration of the companies.

The result was the development of the Fowler Mark 5F crawler, which employed the single-cylinder 2-stroke diesel engine, as used in the Field Marshall series 2, together with Fowler tracks and running gear. With the combined efforts of Marshall and Fowler a prototype crawler was ready for field test work by April 1947. After undergoing vigorous tests it made its first public

Fowler FD3 crawler circa 1944

The Fowler Mark VF crawler

appearance at the Royal Show in Lincoln later that year, along with other products of both companies which incidentally included a Fowler FD3 crawler. The prototype was then returned for further field tests and monitored for any possible flaws in its construction, or overestimation of its maximum overload abilities.

Initially the new crawler was to be named the FD5 but because of the decision to discontinue the FD series, it was considered inappropriate. Finally 5F was agreed upon, but as Fowler used the Roman numeral V to denote the arabic 5 on the front badge, the crawler was soon nicknamed the 'vee F'. By April 1948 it was made ready for a public demonstration, held at St Ives in Cambridge, where six VF crawlers were hurriedly prepared to perform to an audience of distributors and potential customers. Thomas Williams, the Minister of Agriculture, was in attendance and was suitably impressed by the performance of the six crawlers.

The VF was finally ready for release in May 1948. The engine was similar to that used in the Field Marshall series 2 but the transmission had been greatly improved upon. Whereas the series 2 had only three forward speeds and a single

reverse, the VF could boast six forward and two reverse gears. The final drive consisted of two large reduction gears, and to compensate for this additional drive shaft the engine rotation was changed to clockwise. The greater number of gears gave the driver the opportunity to select the appropriate speed for the task in hand. In first gear the VF had an outstanding pull of 10,000 lb.

Production remained at the John Fowler Steam Plough Works at Hunslet, whilst Britannia Works continued to concentrate on fulfilling orders for the series 2. The VF was very popular and was distributed world-wide, either as an agricultural crawler or in bulldozer form. (See Chapter 9 for the continuation of its story.)

Marshalls could clearly see the advantages of the 6-speed gearbox and by the end of 1949 were already looking towards developing a new wheeled tractor. The diesel engine was increasingly seen in the motor tractor and many of Marshalls' competitors already offered a diesel alternative for their tractors. By 1949 Ford, International Harvester, Massey Harris and David Brown had on the market smooth-running multi-cylinder diesel engines with hydraulic 3-point linkage and electric start. This made the

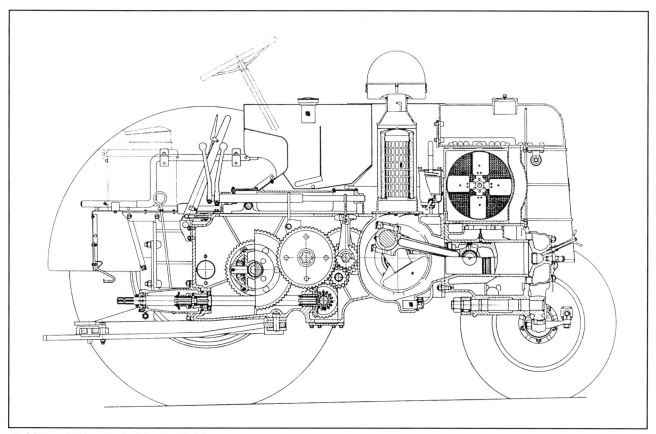

Field Marshall series 3 right-hand side

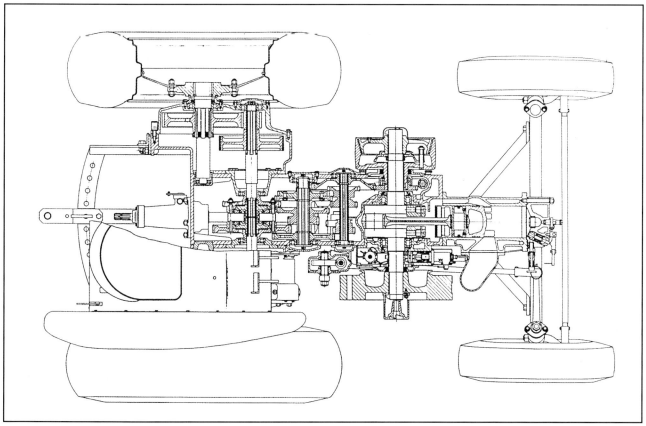

Field Marshall series 3 aerial view

series 2 look rather outdated and crude in comparison.

In the face of such competition, sales of the series 2 in Britain began to decline. The overseas market remained buoyant with good orders still being placed by Canada, France, Africa and Australia. It was obvious, however, that for Marshalls to maintain their foothold abroad, any further development of the series 2 had to encompass the need to haul large implements over huge expanses of land in France, the Canadian prairies and Australian farms. In view of the wide range of working conditions, the 6-speed gearbox as used in the VF was studied with interest. In the summer of 1948 a Fowler VF was despatched to Britannia Works.

It was stripped of its tracks and running gear and given a front axle, wheels and a steering box. This adaption, crude though it was, allowed Marshalls to visualise whether or not they were working along the right lines without bearing the cost of building a full prototype. The experiment was successful and the field test engineers gave glowing reports. It had not escaped the attention of the directors that there were substantial savings to be made in basing their new Field Marshalls on the VF. For instance, money could be saved as parts would be standardised and interchangeable. The cost of retooling and machining would be reduced and the number of wearing spare parts required by distributors for stock would also be less.

By July 1949 two prototype Field Marshalls had been produced and were undergoing strict field and bench test work, under the scrutiny of the top men at Marshalls and Fowlers. By late 1949 the new Field Marshall series 3 was practically ready for release and in early 1950 production was well underway. Marshalls fulfilled their objective of component standardisation, with over 60 per cent of the series 3 parts being interchangeable with the VF.

The sales brochures, produced to herald the arrival of the series 3, boldly defined the advantages of the improvements and stated that it had been designed specifically to satisfy the needs of heavy cultivation world-wide. The series 3 had a far more rugged construction than its forerunner the series 2. The giant 14 in x 30 in rear section tyres with 750 in x 16 in front tyres enhanced the tractor's appearance and was in keeping with some of the robust American tractors.

The water cooling capacity received attention and was increased by $2\frac{1}{2}$ gallons in an attempt to overcome the problems that had been experienced in tractors working in hotter climates; this was an essential improvement for the Australian market. The fuel tank was also increased in capacity to accommodate more fuel for uninterrupted working of vast acreage. The increase in the volume of the fuel and header tank did much to alter the appearance of the tractor, for these changes gave it a far squarer look, and it was fairly easy to distinguish between a series 2 and 3 by the deeper header tank. Another area that underwent revision was the steering box. A far sturdier box had been designed together with a new reconstructed front axle and steering assembly, strengthened to withstand the constant battering from the undulating rough ground. The output of the engine had not been altered, as increased pulling power could be achieved by the greater number of working speeds. The engine had seen little alteration in its build, except for a modification of the air sealing rings in the crankcase. An improvement of the air filtration system, to enhance its performance, was implemented with the proven Burgess air pre-cleaner as a standard feature.

Undoubtedly the VF gearbox used in the series 3 had many of the characteristics of previous Marshall designs, with the exception of the differential bevel wheels. The transmission consisted of spur gears that were situated on transverse shafts, which had been a favoured Marshall layout in the construction of their single-cylinder tractors from the early days of the 15/30. It was very much a derivation of the former steam engine design with both crankshaft and layshafts in parallel, which evenly distributed the bearing loads to either side of the main casing. The 6-speed gear range was accomplished by the provision of a sliding double pinion gear located on the second motion shaft. This meshed with the corresponding gears on each side of the differential unit to provide the required high and low ratio drive. It was literally a 3-speed gearbox with a high and low facility but adequately provided a wider selection of working speeds that varied from 2.6 to 11.3 m.p.h. for road use.

The differential drive was carried to the rear wheel final drive gears by two half shafts and

(Text continues on p.113)

Prototype series 3 Field Marshall undergoing field test work in 1949 (note the absence of the duel fuel filters)

Prototype Field Marshall series 3 at Trent Works 1949 (note the series 2 tractors in the foreground awaiting their final coat of paint)

A prototype series 3 Field Marshall on dynamometer test in the development bay at Britannia Works. The man second from the left is Marshalls' Chief Engineer, Victor Hopkins (note the whiff of steam coming from the header tank and the unusual oil filter housing)

For the price

of a Pint

you can buy enough fuel*

to plough one acre

with the 40 b.h.p.

FIELD-MARSHALL

*Assuming that beer costs 1/2 — 1/6 a pint and diesel fuel from 1/2 to 1/6 a gallon

Is your Fuel Bill as low as this?

 FIELD-MARSHALL SERIES 3 DIESEL TRACTOR

Full details from Marshall Sons & Co., Gainsborough, Lincs.
Telephone: Gainsborough 2301. A PRODUCT OF THE MARSHALL ORGANISATION

Publicity advertisement for Field Marshall series 3 extolling its economic advantages

Introductory advertisement for Field Marshall series 3 tractor

incorporated two large brake drums, which were controlled by an outer band of special oil immersible linings. This provided ample direct braking power that could be applied independently if required, to assist with turning or for general braking. A rear power take-off shaft for driving farm implements became a standard feature on the series 3, as opposed to being an optional extra on its forerunner. It was conveniently centrally mounted, and had a centre line speed of 523 r.p.m. Introduction of legal requirements of drawbar levels had imposed certain restrictions on tractors manufactured in Britain and the series 3 drawbar was designed to meet these requirements. The bars could be adjusted vertically to suit the various depths of cultivation. Attention had been directed towards improving driver comfort, and the series 3 could boast a deep-cushioned upholstered seat, the base of which doubled as a large weatherproof tool box for the storage of tools, starting papers and cartridges. The throttle control lever was relocated beneath the steering wheel to allow easier access, and gave a finer control of the engine speed, since it did not have a ratchet as with the series 2. The independent brake levers were discontinued in favour of pedals and the handbrake lever was repositioned to the left-hand side of the driver. All these improvements made the operator's area less cluttered and since all the controls were within easy reach it simplified driving the tractor considerably.

December 1949 witnessed the release of the first batch of series 3 tractors. This was by no means the official launch. A decision was made to build a stockpile of series 3 tractors before announcing an official release date, in order to cater for those customers already on the waiting list and be in the position to supply on demand.

The first batch released was simply part of the evaluation programme, commencing with serial no. 12001. The majority of these went overseas to Australia and Canada, with only a handful being distributed within Britain. The first production series 3 with serial no. 12001 was retained at Britannia Works and spent all of its life as a developmental tractor, with additions and improvements being carried out prior to the general release of each revision on production tractors. This particular series 3 remained a test tractor until the demise of the Field Marshall in 1957. It was eventually sold and featured many of the components from later tractors, such as the Adrolic 3-point linkage system. It is of interest to note that this tractor is in preservation today and belongs to an enthusiastic British collector from

Series 3 undergoing dynamometer test at Trent Works. Every tractor produced was run on the dynamometer for at least a day to check performance and problems

First production series 3 serial no. 12001 hauling a Grain Marshall 626 combine harvester. This tractor was retained at Britannia Works and constantly used for development work

The Royal Show, Oxford in 1950. The series 3 fitted with a Bray hydra loader makes its debut (note the Union Jack on the front bonnet of the tractor on the left)

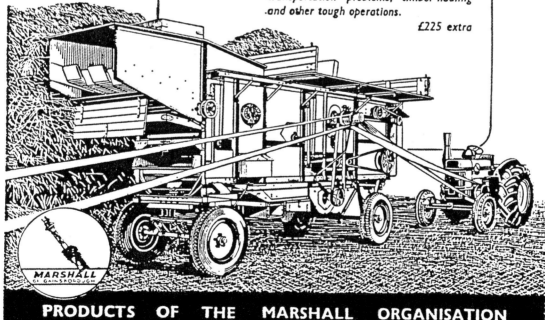
Advert for Field Marshall series 3 and Grain Marshall threshing machine

Yorkshire.

Within weeks of the release of the series 3, problems were apparent in machines that had been shipped to Canada. Customers complained of the tractor's inability to haul loads in its top gear, which the series 2 could comfortably do. When soil conditions were light, tractors could operate implements at high speed, which was essential if the vast acres of prairie land were to be covered. Due to the lightness of the soil and hence the greater use of high speed gears, there were complaints of difficulty in pulling away. Previous owners of the series 2 cited the fact that their old machines were outperforming their new ones. In response, Marshalls sent out service engineers to investigate the problem and the solution was found by reducing the top speed gear from 11.3 to 9.1 m.p.h. After some

instructional guidance from the engineers, Marshall dealers learnt how to select the correct gears for the task in hand and hence improved their demonstrations.

Complaints filtered in from Africa, Australia and Britain, which had also experienced difficulties when pulling a load in top gear. Marshalls decided to carry out installations of the 9.1 m.p.h. speed gear free of charge and many tractors received this modification. All series 3 tractors built after serial no. 12753 received the reduced ratio top speed gears, which provided a lower speed of 9.1 m.p.h. as a standard feature.

Marshalls decided to discontinue the special contractors version and as an alternative offered all the equipment, including an updated winch, available to buy separately. This gave the customer the opportunity to buy the basic tractor

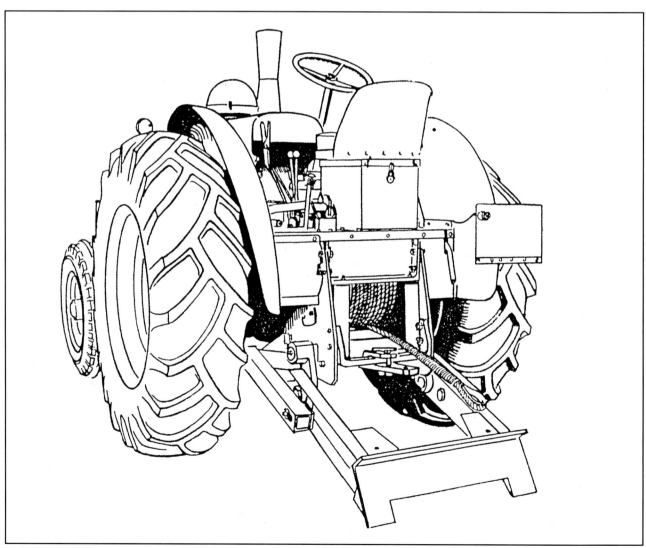

Rear view of series 3 showing the Marshall winch

Field Marshall series 3 showing its abilities as a winch tractor

Field Marshall series 3 with Marshall winch, manoeuvring a rather substantial oak tree trunk

CHAPTER 6

for a mere £718 and add whatever implements were required. The new winch, for example, could be fitted to the basic tractor for an extra £225. Again positioned neatly beneath the driver's platform, it was much sturdier than before and had an increased mean line pull of 11,000 lb. The design of the new winch incorporated the long-awaited free rolling drum, which allowed the operator to manually pull the rope out from the drum and attach it to a load without needing to bring the tractor into close contact. This feature had not been available on the former contractors models and was warmly welcomed. The new winch was also equipped with a ratchet device, which would prevent the load from running away in the event of winch brake failure. The drive to the winch was provided by the centrally mounted power take-off shaft, through a bevel drive gearbox that incorporated a sliding dog clutch for engaging the initial drive. A sprocket mounted on the output shaft supplied a chain drive to the winch drum driving shaft. This driving shaft was in turn mounted on an eccentric bush that could be rotated by a lever to the left-hand side of the driving seat. Pushing the lever forward moved the shaft so that a pinion would engage the internal teeth of the winch drive ring gear and thus commence drive. Obviously, pushing the lever backwards would disengage the drive and leave the drum free rolling, providing the winch brake had been released. The winch brake was of a simple design and was extremely effective. When the brake lever was applied it closed a Ferodo-lined band that surrounded the outer face of the drum and thus maintained a secure hold on the drum and prevented any overrun of the winch rope. The winch drum had 75 yd of ⅝ in steel cable and a retractable speed of 100 ft per minute at 750 r.p.m. under load.

As an optional extra, Marshalls also made available another winch which had been manufactured by

Field Marshall series 3 equipped with Boughton GP18 single speed winch

Series 3 leaving the production line at Britannia Works. Usually the tractors were tow started into life and then driven to Trent Works for testing

an outside company, T & T Boughton of Amersham in Buckinghamshire. Boughton had established themselves as one of Britain's leading winch manufacturers and had already achieved success with their GP17 winch, which had been fitted by distributors on selected Mark I and series 2 Field Marshalls. At the time, Marshalls had not broadcast the success of the Boughton winch for fear of prejudicing sales of their own. It seemed the time was opportune to offer customers a choice. Marshalls advocated the GP18 for the series 3. The Boughton GP range (general purpose) was ideally suited to the needs of the threshing contractor, due to its simple layout and ease of operation in comparison to the Marshall-built unit. It could also be adapted to fit any tractor without the need for any major alterations.

The GP18 was a self-contained unit that was easily attached to the rear of the tractor by means of four large securing brackets. These were conveniently designed to align with the pre-drilled holes in the casing that had been provided for the

Marshall winch. The drive was transmitted from the power take-off shaft into an enclosed chain drive reduction gear and in turn through to a simple crown wheel and pinion drive through to the winch drum.

The operation of the winch was also simple. One single lever situated behind the driver's seat engaged and disengaged the drive, while a separate lever to the left of the driver's seat controlled the winch drum brake. The drum carried a standard 150 ft of ⅝ in wire rope, or an optional 225 ft of ½ in rope. The GP18 was capable of a mean line pull of up to 165,000 lb which was in fact 5000 lb greater than that of the Marshall winch.

In appearance, the Boughton winch was not as well positioned as the Marshall unit, as the winch drum protruded behind the driver's platform, and once the winch anchors were in the travel position this obstructed entry to the driver's platform. This minor inconvenience did not deter customers and there is no doubt that more series 3 tractors left Britannia Works with Boughton winches than with the Marshall unit. One particular farming family from Essex ordered six series 3 tractors all fitted with the Boughton winch.

Customers would often report greater efficiency of the Boughton in service. It was much lower geared than the Marshall, for which snatch blocks were often needed to reduce the line speed and gain a steadier control over the load. If customers were not satisfied with either the Marshall or Boughton winch they could choose one by another manufacturer. This accounts for many series 3 tractors being fitted with Hesford, Cooke, Darlington or Lainchbury winches. These were usually fitted by the distributor or the customer, since the Marshall and Boughton winches were generally installed during the erection of the tractor on the assembly line at Britannia Works.

Marshalls were slow to respond to the idea of providing a 3-point linkage lift system to their tractors. Harry Ferguson designed the first successfully mounted hydraulic controlled implement system, and his revolutionary invention had advanced farm mechanisation a great deal. Many of the leading manufacturers began to see the advantages of the 3-point linkage system as it allowed the tractor and the implement to become one unit, which not only eliminated the problem of providing transport to manoeuvre the tools from field to field but also meant a greater control of the implement via a single lever. By 1950 Ferguson, David Brown and Nuffield had produced tractors with their own version of a 3-point linkage system as standard equipment. It was unfortunate that Marshalls' Board of Directors did not regard the 3-point linkage system as marketable, because the Field Marshall was primarily designed for threshing and heavy cultivation duties, which required the use of heavy trailed implements. The farming public could see the advantages of using a tractor-mounted implement and defected to other manufacturers who could provide a tractor with an hydraulically controlled linkage.

The Adrolic Engineering Company Ltd of Milngavie, in Scotland, had achieved considerable success in designing a hydraulic 3-point linkage system that would fit almost any make of tractor. It was fundamentally a self-contained unit which was easy to install on a Field Marshall. It had been tried on the earlier Mark I and series 2 tractors but had not proven entirely successful.

The system consisted of a single rotary vane hydraulic pump, driven from the tractor's power take-off shaft, with the oil supply coming from a cast reservoir that also housed the lift control unit. A framework attached to the main structure supported the control unit and provided a fixing point for the two lower lift arms. Two control levers — one for lifting and lowering, the other for holding the implement in a set position — made the operation of the unit fairly simple. A levelling box built into the right-hand side drop arm provided any additional adjustment to the lower link arm from the driver's seat.

In a bid to provide the 3-point linkage system for the series 3 and maintain customer interest, Marshalls approached Adrolic and contracted them to provide their universal system as an optional extra to the series 3's standard specification. Adrolic also produced a simple hydraulic supply point for powering hydraulically controlled trailed implements. Again, a rotary vane pump that supplied oil to a double-acting spool block fed through the two self-sealing couplings to the implement. Sales of both the hydraulic lift and auxiliary supply were disappointing, as they were rather crude and did not feature depth or response control that were available on other manufacturers' tractors.

Adrolic were not alone in trying to further the series 3's abilities. W Bray of Hounslow, in Middlesex, made an ambitious attempt to install one of their hydra loaders onto a series 3. Bray already had a close working relationship with Marshalls, as they fitted their bulldozer equipment onto the Fowler VF crawlers. Bray had taken the ruggedness and power of the series 3 into consideration and decided that it would be ideal for providing the skid unit for a loading shovel. In the early 1950s the prototype Field Marshall hydra loader was ready and in July made its first public appearance at the Royal Show in Oxford. Shortly after the show, the hydra loader participated in a number of demonstrations. Nottingham County Council had it on evaluation for a short while but each demonstration was met with bitter disappointment. In a bid to improve the operation of the loader, the position of the hydraulic pump was altered from the rear power take-off shaft and given a direct drive from a

Series 3 equipped with Adrolic 3-point linkage
(Rural History Centre, University of Reading)

sprocket bolted to the engine's flywheel. This modification enabled the operator to raise and lower the boom without disengaging the drive, when the clutch pedal was depressed.

Further attempts to improve the operation of the loader were marred by several disadvantages that came to light. The typical Marshall bounce from the momentum of the single-cylinder engine would jolt the bucket violently when the engine was in low revs, discharging most of the load as well as making for an uneven work surface. The sheer weight alone of the tractor and loader at 5½ tons rendered it almost impossible to steer when the bucket was fully loaded. The most important factor to emerge, however, was the prohibitive cost. The Field Marshall series 3 skid unit retailed at £718, without the additional cost of the loading shovel. Fordson skid units could be bought for almost half the price and for a little extra an electric start diesel engine to boot.

The Marshall Bray hydra loader was returned to Britannia Works, dismissed as an unmarketable item and all further development was ceased. Unlike most of the failed projects that were

usually scrapped for parts, the Marshalls hydra loader spent the rest of its working life at Britannia Works. It was employed in the coal yard to load fuel into the massive boilers which provided heat and energy for the factory.

This was far from the last attempt to utilise the series 3 as an earth-moving machine, for in 1951 Bomford & Evershed Ltd of Evesham, in Kent, adapted their Sapper front mounted bulldozer attachment for the series 3. The basic model consisted of a simple manually operated pump to raise and lower the blade, while the power bulldozer was provided with a power take-off driven hydraulic pump and spool block. A rear mounted scraper blade with an optional power or manual lift was also provided by Bomford. Neither of these was particularly successful though and sales remained disappointing nationwide.

Marshalls decided to expand their range of accessories, which was a clever sales tactic, as not only did this increase profit but it also made the price of a basic tractor more attractive to the farming public. Salesmen were instructed to

Series 3 equipped with hydraulic power take-off

Series 3 demonstrating Fisher Humphries hydraulic trip plough

Bomford Sapper bulldozer fitted to a Field Marshall series 3

stress the advantages of such accessories and Marshalls produced a separate brochure listing the 24 items available, which were as follows:

1. 11 in x 36 in rear wheels to replace the original 14 in x 30 in.
2. Steel wheels with spud and skid rings.
3. Road bands for use with steel wheels.
4. Wheel scrapers for steel or pneumatic wheels.
5. Connecting plate for brake pedals.
6. Standard electric lighting equipment, comprising dynamo, battery, one headlamp, one rear lamp and two side lamps.
7. Colonial electric lighting set, consisting of dynamo, battery, two fixed spotlights and one swivelling spotlight (unsuitable for road use and not available in Britain).
8. Spotlight for standard lighting set.
9. Front push pole bracket.
10. Spring hitch drawbar (export only).
11. Detachable jaw piece for drawbar.
12. Air intake exterior pipe.
13. Spark arrester for exhaust.
14. Driver's cab deluxe.

15. Driver's cab standard.
16. Wiper motor (manually operated).
17. Wiper motor (electrically operated).
18. Set of front bonnet weights.
19. Running hour recorder.
20. Hydroflater.
21. Tyre pressure gauge.
22. Tyre foot pump.
23. Driver's rear view mirror.
24. Power take-off guard.

Several of these optional extras had been available on earlier models and were continued because of their popularity. Some of the accessories had been improved upon, such as the lighting set. Though it still retained its series 2 specification it had been upgraded by using a 6 volt electrical system, which meant that the light beam remained constant and could be used without running the engine. Similarly the standard driver's cab, which was manufactured by Portland, was the same as that used on the series 2, being of solid pressed sheet metal construction and fitted with large side and front glass windscreens. The vibrations produced by the momentum generated by the single-cylinder engine were absorbed by this cab. Every squeak, knock and rattle was amplified to such a degree that it could do considerable damage to the operator's hearing. Unfortunately the driver had little choice other than to risk ear damage or remove the cab and be subjected to bad weather. A cab of sheet steel and canvas construction was later made available. The canvas absorbed a great deal of vibration and the noise was greatly reduced. Another advantage was that the canvas roof and side panels were easily removed and allowed for an open top in fine weather. Very few Field Marshall drivers experienced the comfort that a cab afforded. The landowner who placed the order for a new tractor seldom operated it and consideration for their drivers was minimal.

Some accessories were available that had been designed with the export market in mind. Countries with a warmer climate such as Australia, New Zealand, Canada and India were interested in buying the air intake extension pipe and spark arrester. The spring hitch drawbar was also successful abroad, but its sale in Britain was handicapped by legal stipulations that restricted the maximum height of pull from the drawbar.

In general, Marshalls provided a large range of optional equipment and fulfilled any customer requests. They did not hesitate to modify, improve or even create as the customer desired and on one occasion equipped a series 3 with an air-assisted trailer braking system.

Despite the initial setbacks with the first batch of tractors, Marshalls confidently moved into full production by February 1950. Large consignments were distributed world-wide, particularly to Australia, New Zealand, Canada, India and Africa, all countries with the large land mass which the series 3 had been designed for. Some overseas distributors still held unsold stocks of the series 2 and were in the rare position of being able to offer both. It is interesting to note that some series 2s were being sold abroad as late as 1951, when

Series 3 with Portland cab

stocks were finally depleted.

In Britain sales of the series 3s were relatively slow at first but gradually gained momentum as customer confidence increased. Initially the smallholder considered it too big and cumbersome for use on the average size farm, and there was some criticism from threshing contractors who said that it was not as versatile as the series 2. They found it did not have the power to haul a full set of threshing tackle without reverting to the low speed range and where the modified gears were fitted they still found it lacking. A large proportion of the power generated was absorbed by oil drag in the construction of the final drive gears. Some farming families who had stayed local to Marshall machines since steam days submitted their orders for the series 3, but sales figures reflected that there had been a large scale defection to competitors' models.

The presence of multi-cylinder diesel engines was strong within the tractor industry and other manufacturers could offer smooth running, electric start machines that could be started with the minimum of effort. The hand blistering, back breaking hand cranking technique became a thing of the past and the electric start marked the dawn of a new era in farm mechanisation. Indeed it was an essential requirement for the high compression diesel engines. In late 1951 the Ford Motor company released their Fordson Major E1A tractor that was powered by a 4-cylinder diesel engine and featured electric starting, lighting and 3-point linkage as standard equipment. It retailed at a mere £441, a relatively low price reflecting the advantages of mass production. The Field Marshall was almost twice the price and was already becoming dated, since it did not provide the comforts the Fordson Major afforded. There was competition from other manufacturers too and farmers basking in the new-found wealth of the affluent 1950s were spoilt for choice.

The Morris Motor company had released a diesel version of their Universal tractor in 1950, which also gave Marshalls cause for concern. Fitted with a Perkins L4 engine, it offered the obligatory electric starting and 3-point linkage as standard. Whilst the Nuffield DM4 had some effect on sales of the Field Marshall, its price was prohibitive and this contained its threat. So far as price, reliability and efficiency were concerned, the Fordson Major had cornered the market and

no British manufacturer could compete.

Aware of the growing competition for their home market, Marshalls were not convinced that their faithful single-cylinder engine tractors were ready for retirement. Encouraged by the consistency and constancy of their overseas sales, Marshalls continued production. Sales of the series 3 were particularly rewarding, with exports to France being the greatest. Many Marshall products had been marketed by French agents owned by Thos Ward, such as Société Enterprises d'Industriel Maritime (SEDIM), who had been responsible for distributing hundreds of Field Marshalls throughout France and Europe.

It was the Canadian market that proved to be the most disappointing. Though the initial difficulty with the gear ratio had been rectified, other problems had come to light. Customers complained about starting difficulties in cold weather, and in temperatures as low as minus 26 degrees F the diesel engine could not be coaxed into life. Some enterprising Canadians tried to combat the problem by running their tractors on a cocktail of petrol, paraffin and diesel, which resulted in poor engine performance. In most cases, they reverted to using petrol/paraffin tractors that could perform under these adverse weather conditions. The mass-produced John Deere machines were available as petrol and vaporising oil versions, again at a far more attractive price. Indeed Canadian reaction to the series 3 was so unfavourable that a number were returned unsold and were reallocated to agents in other countries.

Sales of the series 3 were far better in Australia and New Zealand, encouraged to a certain degree by a wide network of distributors providing a sales and back-up service for Marshall and Fowler tractors. One problem was that during the long weeks of shipment, deterioration of paintwork and dented panelwork were commonplace, and this led to an agreement between Marshalls and some distributors to receive their tractors finished in primer only. The distributors would clean off any corrosion caused by the salt water and apply the final coat themselves. This allowed for personal choice, which accounts for an array of colours on a small number of series 3 tractors. A particularly popular colour scheme in certain areas of Australia was red with yellow wheel centre *(see page 131)*.

Destined for export. These wooden boxes were built over the tractor for protection against damage in transit

Throughout the production life of the series 3 the usual modifications filtered through which were geared to improving performance. Minor alterations also occurred to simplify future service or repair work. A particular problem with premature wear became evident in countries where the series 3 was working in dusty environments. Excessive wear in the cylinder bore and in the main bearings was caused by impurities entering the oil reservoir via the oil pump priming handle. The problem was easily overcome as tractors produced after serial no. 13930 received a detachable priming handle, together with a screw-on cover to seal up the pump-driving dog after the handle had been removed.

Recurring problems with oil contamination clearly indicated that further attention was needed in this area. Modifications were made to the dip stick tube, the crankcase and oil filter breather. This apparently eliminated the problem and a modification kit was produced to fit not only existing tractors but also the Mark I and

series 2. The dust inhibition kit was fitted as a standard feature after serial no. 15016.

Among the improvements made to simplify servicing was the redesign of the fan drive pulley. The pulley could be separated and served to reduce the degree of physical strength required when fitting a new belt. During servicing the belt could be tensioned by removing the shims, positioned between the two pulley sheaves, giving a finer adjustment. The adjustable pulley was fitted as standard equipment after serial no. 14000 and a separate kit to fit existing tractors was available for the token sum of £1 5s 2d.

From conception of the very first single-cylinder 2-stroke engine tractor, Marshalls had tried hard to combat the problem of oil emissions from the exhaust pipe, and they had achieved a limited success. It was nonetheless impossible to eradicate the problem due to the very construction of the 2-stroke engine. It was inevitable with any design of a 2-stroke engine, that employed crankcase scavenging, that some oil deposits

Field Marshall series 3 finished in Fowler colours (orange with black lines), Royal Show, Newton Abbot in 1952

would find their way into the combustion chamber via the transfer ports. Other manufacturers such as Lanz, Vierzon and Landini all suffered from the same, if not worse, oil emission problem. Though some attempts had been made to reduce the quantity of emission by trapping the deposits in the exhaust silencer before they were able to escape to the atmosphere, this still remained a minor drawback with the 2-stroke. Other areas that could have compounded the oil problem were investigated, and when it was discovered that a small amount of oil was able to escape past the piston rings, several different formations of piston ring layouts were tried. Four plain chrome piston rings were one such formation but this technique only led to further problems, allowing more oil to pass into the combustion chamber because of the rings' tendency to wear out the cylinder bore prematurely.

Excess oil distribution causing a build-up of oil in the crankcase was the next theory propounded and attention was then concentrated on the lubrication pump. By reducing the amount of oil supplied to the little end and connecting rod bearing, it was thought that the amount of emission would be lessened. Continuous field testing indicated that this did little to control the problem and indeed created further difficulties with engine seizure due to an inadequate oil supply. Any further attempts to control the oil supply were then abandoned and Marshalls were left with no alternative other than to concentrate on reducing the oil emission by improving the waste oil drain facilities incorporated within the exhaust silencer. This problem remained a constant embarrassment until the demise of the single-cylinder diesel engine in 1957.

Early 1950 Field Marshall series 3 (J Bloom)

Although finished in later colours, this is the earliest series 3 tractor, serial no. 12001. It was retained at Marshalls where it continued to receive extensive modifications and development

Rear view of no. 12001, showing fitment of hydraulic 3-point linkage and unusual optional 36 in rear wheel centres

An unusual front axle arrangement fitted to tractor no. 12001

Rear view of Field Marshall series 3 equipped with Marshall heavy duty winch

Field Marshall series 3 equipped with Boughton GP18 winch

Some Field Marshalls received this unusual colour scheme in Australia
(G Shaw)

A 1950 Field Marshall series 3 complete with 6 volt lighting set

CHAPTER 7

In Search of More Power

An additional complaint about the series 3 was its inability to maintain the full 40 h.p. After investigation, results showed that there was a high incidence of customer negligence in executing the maintenance schedules correctly. Even where such procedures had been carried out properly, however, there were instances where performance lacked. It was found that in nearly all these cases, it was the fuel injection system that was at fault. It was discovered that shortly after the delivery of the tractor and within the initial bedding-in process, the injector gradually lost pressure and caused sub-standard engine performance. Once identified, the problem was soon overcome by simply increasing the pressure of the injector above the normal factory setting and allowing for a settle-down period after the tractor's first few hours of work. Complaints of power loss still

continued so Marshalls went on to develop a new injector nozzle that could be fitted to all machines suffering from poor performance. This injector was phased into the assembly line during October 1950, after serial no. 13200.

Competition in the form of the Fordson Major, together with the array of other multi-cylinder diesel tractors on the market, had proven to be somewhat detrimental to the continued success of the Field Marshall. Indeed sales figures in the mid 1950s were in rapid decline in Britain. The consensus amongst the farming community was that it was a little outdated and was past its heyday. In an attempt to protect the narrowing profit margin, Marshalls reduced the tractor's warranty from 12 to 6 months in order to save money on parts and labour, but this did little to curry favour with potential customers. Fortunately

Early series 3A finished in mid Brunswick green

Series 3A in Fowler orange (note the hour meter situated behind the clutch pulley)
(Rural History Centre, University of Reading)

sales continued to be buoyant abroad, with overseas exports to France, Spain, Australia and New Zealand still accounting for more than a quarter of the yearly production figures, as the multi-cylinder tractor had not yet had an effect on overseas trade. Critical feedback from distributors abroad was taken very seriously by Marshalls. They could not afford to lose their foothold in the overseas market and took on board the calls for an improved engine output with easier starting techniques. Fear of declining export sales stopped the complacency that Marshalls had been guilty of and spurred them on to a radical revamp of the Field Marshall.

Marshalls called upon the services of their Chief Engine Development Engineer, Victor Hopkins, to fulfil the criteria demanded: a minimum output of 40 h.p. under a full load without any deviation. Hopkins was familiar with the single-cylinder engine, having made a major contribution during the initial development stages of the series 3 in 1949. Indeed his experience in the field of progressive development of the diesel engine was

unsurpassed and he had shared his genius with other top engineers Frank Perkins and Harry Ricardo. Marshalls had full confidence in Hopkins to achieve their objectives, which included finding a solution to the problem of sudden piston seizure and scuffing of the cylinder bore.

To achieve an improved engine output, Hopkins' solution was to upgrade the fuel injection system. By simply installing a new injector nozzle and increasing the atomising pressure to 2500 p.s.i., a constant 40 h.p. was obtained. The fuel pump cam was also re-profiled to give a faster injection rate and a slower return to prevent anti-reverse running. Several alterations were made to other areas of the fuel supply system, one of them being a new delivery pipe that incorporated a surge vessel that would counteract hesitation when the sudden need for an immediate response was required.

To eliminate the problem of piston seizure, Hopkins introduced a 2-part piston ring comprising a wide angular chamber ring and a narrow rectangular sealing ring. Later known as the fire ring, this arrangement helped to disperse the excess heat generated by the piston. He also introduced the use of self-cleaning taper sided rings for the remaining formation. These dispersed the excess carbon deposits that had been the cause of sticking rings and scuffing cylinder walls.

The importance of Victor Hopkins' work in the revamping programme cannot be overstated. Not only did he improve output, but also fuel consumption. In addition to this, he took account of the need to simplify routine service work by altering the access to the vaporising locking screw and later by the provision of a new main air filter element to replace the antiquated coconut fibre packed device that had been in use since 1936 with the 18/30.

A conversion kit was made available to fit existing series 3 tractors that were in need of an engine overhaul. Many of the machines that received these C kits were given a new lease of life, thanks to Hopkins' supremacy in the world of diesel engineering.

In September 1952, Marshalls released a series of service bulletins to their distributors and agents, in order to inform them of the introduction of the new upgraded engine. These bulletins also listed further improvements and built-in modifications that were to feature in tractors produced after serial no. 15207. Although a major proportion of the revamping programme had been geared towards improved engine performance, there were several other areas that received alterations. For example, the power take-off shaft had an improved bevel drive gear with roller bearings replacing the former bushed shaft. As a cost-cutting exercise, Marshalls decided to make the power take-off shaft an additional extra and offered it for sale at £25. The phasing in of other improvements

A 3A with Field Marshall Mark I tractor awning. These awnings or rag-tops were usually fitted to later Field Marshall tractors for export only

continued, and in November 1952 tractors produced after serial no. 15662 received a pressurised cooling system to enhance the engine's cooling efficiency.

In order to make the farming public aware of these alterations and modifications to the series 3, Marshalls decided that the extent of improvements justified giving the new tractor a separate identity and so the series 3A was born. Shortly after serial no. 15662, the tractors on the production line were finished in Fowler orange, instead of the usual green that all Marshalls tractors had been painted since the conception of the 12/20 in 1934. The sudden change to bright orange failed to gain immediate acceptance. Indeed there were several incidences of customers refusing to accept delivery of their new 3A and ordering the driver to return it to be repainted in Brunswick green.

The series 3A was not the first Marshall product to be finished in Fowlers' colours. Whenever Marshalls and Fowlers exhibited their products jointly, it was common practice for some Marshall products to be painted in Fowler orange complete with black lines.

The 3A continued to be improved upon throughout production. Recurring problems with the gear selector mechanism jamming resulted in a modified selector fork, which had a wider slot to accommodate the selector pawl. The 3As produced after February 1955 and commencing with serial no. 16768 received the improved selector. It also became apparent that a lack of performance was caused by the inevitable build-up of excess carbon deposits in the silencer. Those customers who regularly maintained their tractor would remove the silencer and burn out the deposits by setting fire to oil-soaked rags. This did not remove all the carbon deposits and a sizeable remainder was always left in the silencer which

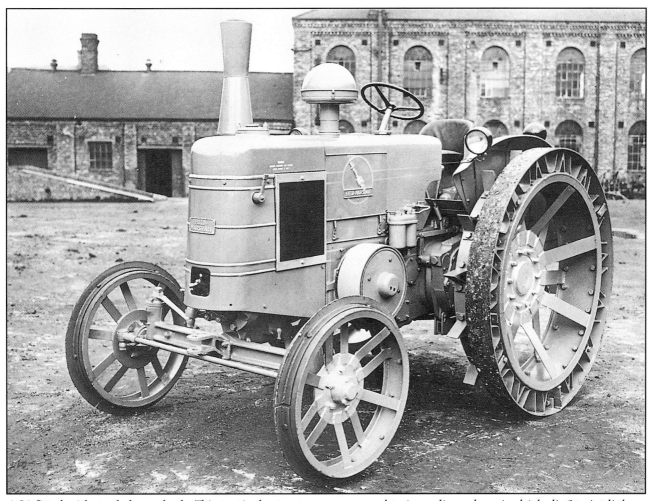

A 3A fitted with spade lugg wheels. This particular tractor was exported to Australia and received Adrolic 3-point linkage (note the air intake extension pipe) (Rural History Centre, University of Reading)

A 3A with Marshall winch, anchors lowered

would build up again. It was not uncommon for the silencer to eventually catch fire, especially if no maintenance had been carried out and the deposits had been left to mount up. If the tractor was hauling a wooden threshing machine, or was in close proximity to a straw rick, the possibility of the silencer suddenly igniting was potentially very dangerous. Marshalls realised that preventative measures were called for and set about improving access to the silencer in order to facilitate cleaning. In January 1955, commencing with serial no. 16808, the new silencer was fitted in two sections which could be separated simply by removing a ring of bolts. Made by Burgess, this silencer was so successful that from September 1955 it became available as a spares item for application to the Mark I, series 2 and series 3 tractors.

The optional extra equipment available for the series 3A remained virtually unchanged from that of the series 3, except that the power take-off shaft became optional as opposed to a standard

feature. The only other major difference was the availability of the 24 volt electric starting equipment, which again was purely optional. Marshalls had been aware for some time that the provision of an alternative starting device would be a marketable asset and had been looking for a suitable method since conception of the series 3, back in 1950. Competitors such as Nuffield and Ford offered electric starting equipment as a standard feature, and Marshalls were well aware that the Field Marshall's starting techniques were not only crude and outdated but also lost them potential sales. The cartridge starting system had been a simple and effective alternative but still left much to be desired. There was the off-putting extra cost involved in buying a supply of cartridges, not to mention their all too frequent malfunctioning due to incorrect storage. The safety aspect was questionable and was a deterrent to the majority of potential customers.

Over the years Marshalls tried several other techniques, one of which was the inertia starting system. This involved the use of a large recoiling spring that was wound manually by a handle to a sufficient pressure to generate enough power to turn the engine over. The pinion shaft would then engage a ring gear on the outer face of the flywheel. The developmental team were keen to experiment with this fairly simple system, so a suitably sized inertia unit was acquired and after a number of modifications and structural alterations it was fitted onto a series 3 tractor. This system did not meet with success, as more effort was required to wind up the inertia motor than was needed to start the tractor in the conventional way with the starting handle. All further experimentations with the inertia system were therefore abandoned.

Marshalls combed the engineering world for other new developments. The Bryce Fuel Injection company of Staines, in Middlesex, appeared at first to have the solution. Bryce had finalised the development of a Berger hydraulically operated self-starting system, that could be adopted to fit almost any build of motor

engine. The system consisted of a complicated arrangement involving the use of a sealed pressurised accumulator fitted with a diaphragm. Hydraulic fluid forced into the lower part of the accumulator, by way of a hand-operated pump, compressed the air at the back of the diaphragm to approximately 4000 lb per square inch. The diaphragm completely separated the air from the fluid and maintained the pressure until it was released into the two reciprocal hydraulic cylinders, each of which contained a piston rack which engaged with a simple pinion. The pinion was integral with a toothed dog that engaged a corresponding dog located on the engine's crankshaft. Once sufficient pressure had been achieved in the accumulator, this stored energy could be released by a control lever, through to the piston heads of each cylinder. The pistons in turn would then be generated forward and engage each rack onto the corresponding drive pinion mounted onto the crankshaft. When full pressure was applied it would provide enough torque to rotate the crankshaft at a sufficient

Bryce Berger hydraulic starting equipment

speed to start the engine.

Greatly encouraged by initial tests, Marshalls bought the unit from Bryce to be fitted to a series 3 development tractor. After considerable effort constructing the framework to accommodate the drive motors, hydraulic tank, accumulator and control valve, together with modifying the end of the crankshaft so that it could receive a drive pinion, the Bryce Berger hydraulic starter was finally ready for field testing. It had a qualified success in that it generated enough power to start the Field Marshall but only if the decompression wheel had been set at its limit. Taking into consideration the cost of installing the starting system and the fact that the general operation of the tractor was impeded somewhat by all the extra apparatus required by the hydraulic starting mechanism, Marshalls aborted any further development.

Gradually Marshalls realised that they were wasting their time trying to find a feasible alternative and submitted to the supremacy of the electric start system. The unconventional design of the single cylinder ensured that it would not be a simple procedure to incorporate the starting equipment, and a certain amount of modification was essential. Marshalls had enjoyed a business relationship with the CAV company of Acton in London for several years, having bought in their lighting equipment for the Field Marshall. CAV had earnt a reputation for designing electric lighting, starting and charging equipment for car, commercial and industrial vehicles.

After a series of meetings a Field Marshall series 3 was despatched to the CAV works at Acton along with selected Marshall engineers. After a period of intense deliberation between

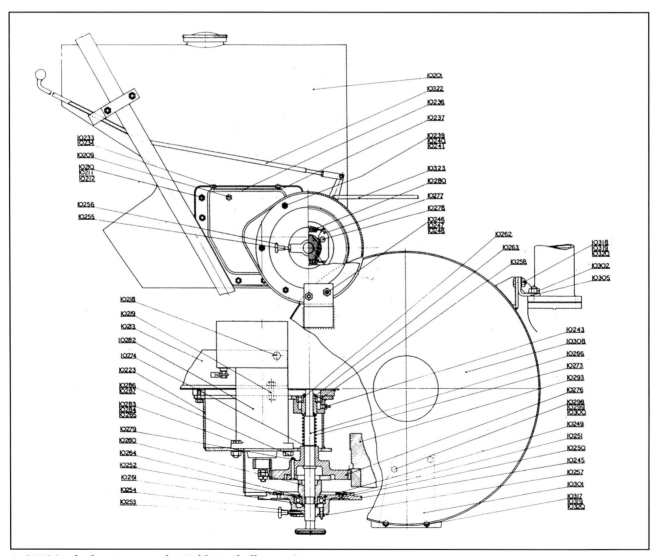

A CAV 24 volt electric starter for Field Marshall series 3A

both companies' engineering teams, a system was found that would not require any extensive alteration to the structural build of the tractor. Ironically, the installation of the self-starting equipment proved to be far less complicated and costly than previous attempts had been. The only areas in the tractor's construction that needed modification were the fuel tank, which had to be modified to accommodate a very large axial starter motor, and the provision of a corresponding ring fitted to the outer face of the flywheel. To generate sufficient momentum to rotate the crankshaft at the required speed to start the engine necessitated the use of a 24 volt electric start system. Most other electric starting systems at that time required only 6 volts to start conventional engines. The toolbox situated on the rear platform beneath the driver's seat was increased in diameter to house the four batteries required to provide the electric power for the starter motor. A simple push button, located centrally beneath the rear section of the fuel tank, was all

that was required to start the engine. As the hand and cartridge systems could still be used as complementary methods to the electric start, the operator was spoilt for choice with three alternative starting methods.

Thrilled with having successfully incorporated the electric start system and with far less structural alteration than they had deemed necessary, Marshalls released details to be included in the additional equipment data and waited for the orders to come rolling in. Disappointment followed, however, as although the system was efficient, the prohibitive price was a deterrent. In 1953 an electric starting kit cost £210 and a standard series 3A £845, twice the price of a new Fordson Major. It is easy to understand why the public response was so poor. The cost of the kit and a standard 3A came to an astounding £1055, which was far in excess of the average farmer's budget. For a tractor that was increasingly becoming outdated in the face of new technology, the price was undoubtedly steep. Even the most stalwart

Early 3A with CAV 24 volt electric starter   (Rural History Centre, University of Reading)

Rear view of 3A with electric starter, showing enlarged battery box beneath driver's seat

Marshall customers baulked at the cost, which resulted in only a handful of electric start Field Marshalls being sold. Although exact figures of production are unavailable, it is believed that no more than 12 series 3As received this device and today's preservation movement bears witness to this by recording the existence of only five survivors: two in Britain, two in Australia and one in France.

Despite continual modifications and uprating of the 3A, its slipping sales record was a clear indication that it had not changed sufficiently. Potential customers remained unimpressed, especially when faced with the wide array of choice from other manufacturers, chiefly Fordson. There was competition from other sources too, as rival manufacturers had been quick to respond to the threat of the Fordson Major and the market was saturated with new models from Massey Ferguson, International and David Brown. These were all companies that had benefitted from the advancement in tractor technology so that electric

start and 3-point linkage were being offered as the norm. Marshalls had to be realistic: their single-cylinder engine had become dated. A restructuring of pricing policy to offer to the public at a more competitive price would simply have meant a substantial loss on each machine produced, so thin was the profit margin already. Reluctantly the Board of Directors passed a motion to withdraw their Field Marshall, the tractor that had served them well for 30 years but could not compete with fast-moving technological advances.

The last recorded Field Marshall 3A to leave Britannia Works was serial no. 17331, in February 1957. This machine, fitted with a Marshall winch and full lighting equipment, was sold through Bomford to a customer in the Cotswold region of Britain. Rumours have dissipated throughout the preservation world for many years concerning a small number of 3As that were built after the last recorded tractor, including one that was constructed from spare parts to special order in

A 3A with CAV, lights, electric starter and Marshall winch at Trent Works

A 3A prepared for shipping to Australia. The final coat of paint was applied by the area distributor

Wooden mock-up of Field Marshall series 4   (Rural History Centre, University of Reading)

the early 1960s. To date, however, no concrete evidence has come to light to confirm that any further 3As were made after serial no. 17331, and it simply remains speculation.

There are many theoretical arguments as to how much longer Marshalls could have held on to the single-cylinder engine tractor. Drawing comparisons with Lanz, had the Field Marshall been able to offer a wider range of horsepower and more versatility, one can assume it could have kept hold of its share of the market. Lanz enjoyed success with their single-cylinder tractors up until the mid 1960s but comparisons with Lanz have to be tempered by the fact that 3-point linkage and electric starting were provided from as early as 1949, not to mention that Lanz produced a far greater range of single-cylinder machines. The vibration caused by the nature of a single-cylinder machine was also tackled by Lanz, who achieved a noticeable reduction by using a lighter piston

made of aluminium.

Had Marshalls copied some of the German company's ideas and applied them earlier during the production years of the Field Marshall, maybe they would have had more success. Indeed there is evidence that the drawing offices at Britannia Works had been commissioned to commence work on a new tractor based on the Lanz principle in 1955 but it was by then too late. The tractor in its preparatory stage was undoubtedly the uncrowned successor to the 3A and would have been called the Field Marshall series 4. Had this machine succeeded into production it would most certainly have featured electric starting, 3-point linkage, a glow plug instead of ignition paper, adjustable axles for row crop work and greater power due to the implementation of a Rootes blower. The series 4 did not progress any further than the drawing board and a wooden mock-up model, as the

The 3A with colonial lighting set

Sectional 3A, prepared by Marshall apprentices, on display at the Royal Smithfield Show, Earls Court, London in 1952
(Rural History Centre, University of Reading)

Display of Marshall and Fowler machinery at the 1953 Royal Smithfield Show, Earls Court, London

design team were engaged upon a totally new project. In collaboration with Marshalls' sister company John Fowler, two new tractors were already well into development by 1954.

In January 1953, several Marshall directors had been sent overseas to try to discover the reasons why sales of the 3A had been somewhat disappointing. They determined that the mass cultivation in the large prairie countries of Australia and Canada necessitated the use of large soil engaging implements and required power at the drawbar which was far beyond the capabilities of the 40 h.p. Field Marshall. A new age of farm mechanisation had dawned, bringing with it a new breed of high powered giant tractors that could cope with high acreage output. Massey Harris, John Deere, Case, International, Allis-Chalmers and Minneapolis Moline were among the foreign manufacturers to offer power exceeding 50 h.p. and continued to develop output with the aid of turbo chargers, superchargers

Mock-up model of a Field Marshall series 4
(C Payne)

and even implemented 6-cylinder engines. It was obvious the Field Marshall was simply dwarfed in size, performance and efficiency against these foreign giants. It made the need for a new breed of Marshall tractor all the more pressing.

Field Marshall series 3A equipped with 24 volt electric starter

At the right is almost the first Field Marshall Mark I, manufactured in June 1945, serial no. 2001. Beside it is the last record-ed Field Marshall series 3A no. 17331   (J Bloom)

Field Marshall series 3A equipped with a French 3-point linkage system

CHAPTER 8
Development Ahead of Time

Marshalls' association with the Fowler company proved extremely beneficial, as Marshalls drew from their expertise. Fowlers were in the production run of their famous Challenger range of crawler tractors, which were of unit construction. For simplicity and ease of access during servicing, the engine transmission and final drives were attached to a heavy duty, hull-shaped chassis. The new Marshall machine being developed was to be constructed in a similar manner with utilisation of as many of the Challenger components as possible to save on costs. Fowlers had bought their engines from outside suppliers for their higher horsepower Challenger range, rather than spending time and money in developing their own. By doing so they had formed a good business relationship with the engine companies Henry Meadows Ltd of

Wolverhampton and Leyland from Lancashire, both of which had been providing the power units for the Challenger Mark II, III and IV crawlers.

The Challenger Mark I crawler had received the vertical 2-cylinder 2-stroke Marshall ED5 engine that had been the brainchild of Chief Engineer Victor Hopkins. This engine was considered as a suitable power source for the new tractor, since it had been designed to reach 50 h.p. and had the capability of 80 h.p. by the simple process of increasing the volume of the cylinder and upgrading the fuel injection system. It was a simple 2-stroke with crankcase scavenging, and it also employed a Rootes blower to achieve the top-end performance. However, when fitted to the Challenger I, the ED5 demonstrated some difficulties with oil emission, high oil consumption and poor starting and was considered too

Fowler Challenger I with Marshall twin-cylinder 50 h.p. 2-stroke diesel engine

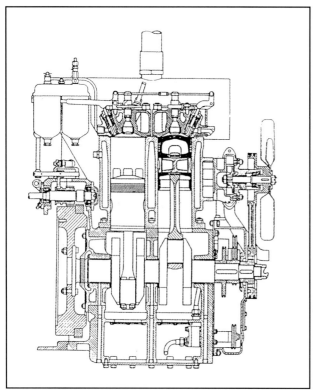

Marshall ED5 2-cylinder 2-stroke diesel engine

problematic to continue with. Withdrawn from service, the ED5 was replaced by a Leyland engine on later Challenger models.

The engine chosen for the new tractor on the trestles at Britannia Works was a Meadows 4DC330 4-cylinder 4-stroke diesel, which was capable of developing 65 b.h.p. at a maximum governed speed of 1600 r.p.m. After installation and remedial structural work were completed, the tractor was despatched for field testing at the disused Skellingthorpe airfield near Lincoln in October 1953.

The appearance of this new machine was strikingly different from that of its forerunner the Field Marshall, and the close relationship to the Fowler Challenger crawler was apparent. At first the new tractor was to be called the Field Marshall series 5 but this was considered too unimaginative. Since it had been designed specifically to compete against the large powerful tractors that were working the prairie lands of Australia, Canada and France, a more appropriate name was finally chosen, the MP4, the Marshall Prairie 4-cylinder.

Prototype MP4 in preparation at Britannia Works 1953
(Rural History Centre, University of Reading)

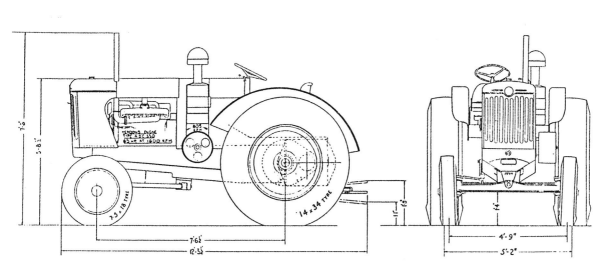

ENGINE   Meadows 4DC330 4 Cyl. 4 stroke, 331 cu. in. (5430 c.c.) displacement. Compression Ignition Oil Engine developing 65 Brake H.P. at 1600 R.P.M. max. governed speed.
Water cooling by radiator and fan with pump circulation.
Electric starting.

CLUTCH   14" Borg & Beck dry single plate, pedal controlled with hand control at rear of tractor.

GEARBOX   6 speeds forward and 2 reverse. Single ball mounted lever control for all speeds with separate lever for reverse.

ESTIMATED OPERATING DRAWBAR PULLS
AND SPEEDS —

Speed Range AG.

		lbs.	m.p.h.	Km/hour
Forward	1st.	6,000	2.13	3.43
	2nd.	5,700	3.38	5.45
	3rd.	4,700	4.15	6.67
	4th.	3,700	5.15	8.3
	5th.	1,840	9.5	15.3
	6th.	1,100	14.8	23.8
Reverse	1st.	—	3.1	5.0
	2nd.	—	4.8	7.7

Max. Sustained Pull 6,500 lbs.

ALTERNATIVE
Speed Range IND.

		lbs.	m.p.h.	Km/hour
Forward	1st.	6,000	2.47	3.98
	2nd.	5,700	3.38	5.45
	3rd.	4,100	4.8	7.7
	4th.	2,900	6.7	10.8
	5th.	1,840	9.5	15.3
	6th.	1,100	14.8	23.8
Reverse	1st.	—	3.6	5.8
	2nd.	—	4.8	7.7

Max. Sustained Pull 6,500 lbs.

Note:—The above estimated speeds and pulls are with water ballasted 14 x 34 rear tyres on dry level tarmacadam.

TYRES   Rear   14.00 — 34
Front   7.50 — 18

DRAWBAR   Swing type adjustable for height
Height from ground   11" — 21"
Width of swing 32"

BRAKES   Contracting band, acting on 15" dia. drums on differential shafts, enclosed in gearbox. Ratio diff. shafts to rear axle 4.93/1. Brakes controlled by independent pedals, and by hand lever simultaneously via compensating gear.

OVERALL DIMENSIONS

Wheel Base	...	90¼"
Overall length	...	147½"
„ width	...	78½"
„ height	...	68½" to top of radiator
		90" to top of exhaust
Wheel track (rear)	...	62"
„ „ (front)	...	57"
Ground clearance	...	15½"

Weight in working order (without water ballast in tyres) ... ... 7800 lbs. (approx)
Weight including water ballast ... ... 9000 lbs. (approx)

OPTIONAL EXTRAS:
BELT PULLEY

     14¾" dia. x 8½" face, controlled by main clutch. 805 r.p.m. giving belt speed 3100 ft/min. Rated Belt H.P. 60.

P.T.O.   Controlled by main clutch driven from input shaft of gearbox.
1⅜" — 6 spline (B.S. 1495) shaft, clockwise from rear 30" above ground, ¼" to right of tractor centre line, shaft end 13" forward of drawbar hitch-pin. Speed 725 r.p.m. with engine at 1600 r.p.m. 544 r.p.m. with engine at 1200 r.p.m. (this corresponds with a travelling speed of 1.6 m.p.h. (2.58 Km/hour in 1st gear of speed range A.G.)

In pursuance of this company's policy of constant development, the right is reserved to depart, without notice, from any detail illustrated or specified in this leaflet. without incurring the obligation to provide such modifications on machines previously delivered.

MARSHALL, SONS AND COMPANY LIMITED, GAINSBOROUGH, LINCS., ENGLAND

Telephone: Gainsborough 2301   Telegrams: Marshalls, Gainsborough

Provisional specification for prototype MP4 tractor

The MP4 was subjected to arduous and extensive field testing and in one period worked continually for two weeks, stopping only for refuelling and general checks. The extensiveness of the trials was a result of a directive from the Marshall board as they wished their new tractor not only to compete with but to excel over their foreign competitors. On a financial note, the directors were only too aware that the company could ill-afford any failures. The MP4 certainly looked the part with a total length of 12 ft 3½ in, and it stood 5 ft 8 in tall at the top of the radiator. With the Meadows engine snugly positioned into the chassis, the line of drive was taken through to the transmission via an intermediate prop shaft fitted with layrub couplings and connected to the first motion shaft in the gearbox. Two variations of gearbox were available, industrial and agricultural, each offering the wide range of six forward and two reverse gears. The industrial gearbox was provided with slightly faster speeds between ranges and equalled the agricultural gearbox top speed of 14.8 m.p.h.

The large final drive and differential housing were situated to the rear of the chassis and were contained within their own separate casing. The line of drive to the differential had been taken directly through a bevel pinion output shaft at the rear of the gearbox and meshed correspondingly into the crown wheel. The drive through to the rear wheels was very much the same principle as used in the Field Marshall series 3 and 3A tractors and employed a further reduction to the rear axles, with the use of large bull gears, independent differential and axle shafts.

The driving arrangement was also similar to that of the Field Marshall, having the driver's seat and controls offset to the right-hand side of the platform. The selection of gears was totally different. The main lever could select a range of six forward speeds, while a second separate lever controlled forward and reverse motions of the tractor and permitted the use of first and second gears only if reverse had been selected.

Whilst the first MP4 was undergoing field testing, another prototype was already in preparation but this second tractor was spared the gruelling trials and spent the majority of its time performing stationary tests on the dynamometer to measure power take-off output. Thereafter it was prepared for publicity and

An MP4 on field test work on the disused Skellingthorpe airfield, Lincolnshire in 1954
(A Halstead)

An MP4 serial no. 2 prepared for publicity shots at Trent Works 1954

Another view of the MP4 serial no. 2 from the left-hand side at Trent Works 1954

marketing requirements by receiving a finishing coat of Fowler orange.

With the field test work accomplished with satisfactory results, the MP4 came a stage closer to full scale production. A specification pamphlet was produced and distributed to all Marshall agents, listing the technical data and performance details. Although the Meadows engine had performed exceedingly well, doubts had been raised about its capabilities to compete with the large 6-cylinder engines of the American machines. Marshalls did not want to find themselves in a situation where their new tractor was struggling against the competition, either in the present or in the near future. Following an overnight decision, full scale production was postponed whilst another engine was tried.

As mentioned previously, Fowlers had used engines from outside companies for some time in their Challenger crawler range and enjoyed a good relationship with both Leyland and Meadows, which was further cemented when Fowlers opted to replace the troublesome Marshall ED5 engine with the 6-cylinder Leyland

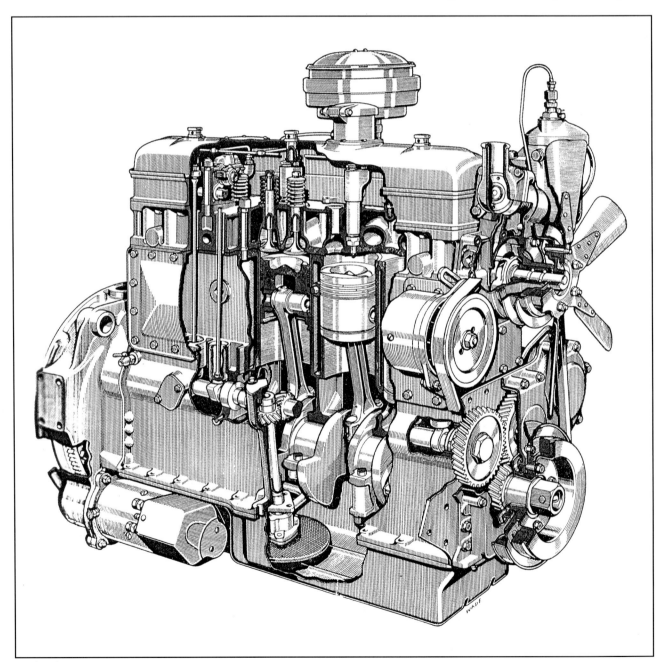

Leyland AU350 engine

Prototype MP6 under construction in Britannia Works 1954

AU350 unit in their Challenger Mark 1 crawler. Leyland took advantage of their liaison with Fowlers and offered Marshalls their AU350 at a far more competitive price than the Meadows engine. After negotiations, Leyland delivered one of their engines to Britannia Works, where the Meadows engine was removed from one of the MP4 prototypes and replaced by the Leyland. The engine supplied was slightly different from that fitted to the Challenger Mark 1 crawler, as it had been uprated to produce a full 70 h.p. and received the identification of UE350.

After receiving the new engine the machine resumed field test work to assess the feasibility of the Leyland power unit. The installation of the UE350 had not been a simple matter. As it was $3^{1}/_{2}$ in longer than the Meadows, the structural hull had to be modified and the front axle needed to be altered to accommodate the heavier weight load. On test, the Leyland certainly proved itself against the Meadows. The fact that it was a

Prototype pre-production MP6 tractor

6-cylinder engine not only improved upon the power output but also provided smoother operation and was far quieter. Marshalls felt more confident that they had a tractor capable of holding its own against their American cousins. On the strength of the new engine's success a further

Prototype MP6 undergoing field test work in 1955
(Rural History Centre, University of Reading)

Pre-production MP6 prepared for its official release in 1954

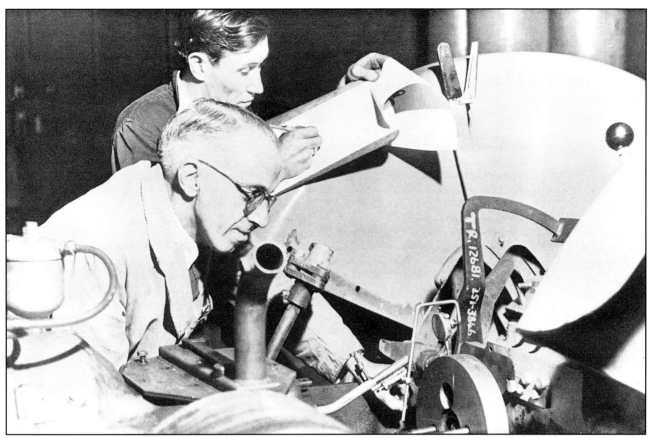

Prototype MP6 being stripped and inspected after undergoing many arduous hours of testing

Works line drawing of production MP6 with revised front grille

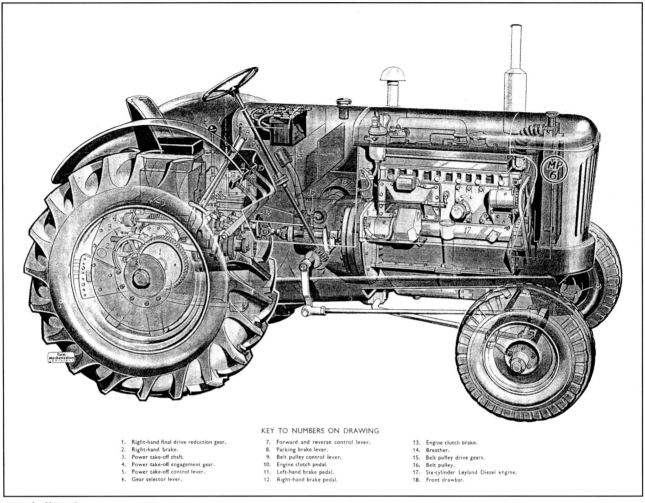

KEY TO NUMBERS ON DRAWING

1. Right-hand final drive reduction gear.	7. Forward and reverse control lever.	13. Engine clutch brake.
2. Right-hand brake.	8. Parking brake lever.	14. Breather.
3. Power take-off shaft.	9. Belt pulley control lever.	15. Belt pulley drive gears.
4. Power take-off engagement gear.	10. Engine clutch pedal.	16. Belt pulley.
5. Power take-off control lever.	11. Left-hand brake pedal.	17. Six-cylinder Leyland Diesel engine.
6. Gear selector lever.	12. Right-hand brake pedal.	18. Front drawbar.

Marshall MP6

supply was ordered and a second MP4 was stripped of the Meadows and given the UE350. A third tractor, still in the process of erection, was automatically fitted with the Leyland and was announced in the farming press. The MP6 had arrived.

The MP6 made its first public appearance in November 1954, at the Public Works Exhibition held at Olympia in London, and its second at the Royal Smithfield Show, Earls Court in London the following month. On these occasions the MP6 took centre stage and interest was immense. Never before had the viewing public seen such a large wheeled tractor, which was certainly the largest on the market in Britain. Accordingly, it had a heavy price tag and retailed at £1400.

Although the MP6 was officially released in 1954, it did not become available until two years later. During this time the three prototypes were submitted to an evaluation programme. Two were retained in Britain while the third was despatched

to Australia, in order to gather vital feedback as to its performance in hotter climates. It was especially important that it should perform well in Australia, since the MP6 had been specifically designed for the cultivation of large areas of land. The two tractors that remained in Britain were used mainly as demonstration units, performing at agricultural shows and displaying the advantages of large scale farming with farm implements that were normally only suitable with the use of large crawler tractors. One of the tractors was despatched to the NIAE, where it underwent the usual test procedures and was duly awarded the British Standard agricultural tractor test no. BS/NIAE/56/4 in April 1956.

Several theories are cited as to why the MP6 was not on the market until nearly two years after its first public appearance. A shortage in supplies of the Leyland engine is one reputed possibility. It is more likely that Marshalls experienced a number of set-backs during the field test work

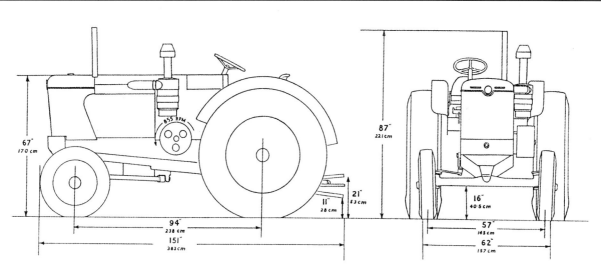

ENGINE

Leyland type U/E 350. 6 Cylinder. 4 Stroke. 351 cu. in. (5760 c.c.). displacement, Compression Ignition Oil Engine developing 70 B.H.P. at 1700 R.P.M. Max. governed speed.

Water Cooling by radiator and fan with pump circulation· Electric starting.

CLUTCH

14" Borg & Beck dry single plate, pedal operated.

GEARBOX

6 speeds forward and 2 reverse. Single ball mounted lever control for all speeds, with separate lever for reverse.

OPERATING DRAWBAR PULLS AND RATED SPEEDS (with engine 1700 R.P.M.)

		lbs.	kg.	m.p.h.	Km/hour
Forward	1st	6500	2940	1.71	2.75
	2nd	6000	2700	3.0	4.83
	3rd	4800	2180	4.06	6.55
	4th	4400	2000	5.06	8.15
	5th	2800	1270	7.55	12.20
	6th	1500	680	14.60	23.50
Reverse	1st	—	—	3.06	4.92
	2nd	—	—	5.32	8.57

Note.—Above speeds and pulls are with water ballasted 14 x 34 rear tyres on dry level Tarmacadam.

TYRES

Rear   14.00 — 34
Front   7.50 — 18

DRAWBAR

Swinging type adjustable for height. Height from ground 11"—21" (28 cm. — 53 cm.).
Width of swing 32" (81 cm.).

BRAKES

Totally enclosed, contracting bands, acting on 15" dia. drums fitted to differential shafts which have 4.93/1 ratio to rear axles. Brakes independently controlled by pedals and simultaneously by hand lever through compensating gear.

OVERALL DIMENSIONS

Wheelbase	...	... 94" or 114¾"	238	cm. or 290.7cm.
Overall Length ...		...151"	383	,,
,, Width ...		... 78½"	200	,,
,, Height to top				
	of radiator	... 67"	170	,,
,, ,, to top				
	of exhaust	... 87"	221	,,
Wheel track rear		... 62" or 80"	157.5	,, or 203 cm. (by reversing wheels)
Wheel track front		... 57"	145	,,
Ground clearance		... 16"	40.5	,,
Weight in working order (without water ballast in tyres)	...	...	8150 lbs. approx.	3700 kg.
Weight (including water ballast)	...	...	9500 lbs. approx.	4300 kg.

OPTIONAL EXTRAS

Belt Pulley. 13⅞" dia x 8½" face (35 cm. x 21.6 cm.), controlled by main clutch. 855 R.P.M. giving belt speed 3100 ft./min. (950 metres/min.).

Power Take-off. 1¾" dia. (4.45 cm.) 6 spline shaft. Clockwise from rear. 29½" (75 cm.) from ground, 1⅛" (2.85 cm.) to right of tractor centre line, shaft end 12" (30.5 cm.) forward of drawbar hitch pin. Speed 544 R.P.M. with engine at 1700 R.P.M.

Wheel Weights. Cast Iron ballast weights up to 900 lbs. (400 kg.) per wheel.

Electric Lights. 12 volt lighting sets for road and/or field work.

APPROXIMATE SHIPPING SPECIFICATION

	Length	Breadth	Height	Cwts.	Kgs.
Protected on wheels ...	12'7" 383.5 cm.	6'7" 200.7 cm.	6'4" 193.1 cm.	70	3550
Fully packed	11'6" 350.5 cm.	6'7" 200.7 cm.	5'3" 160 cm.	76	3860
Also one pair hind wheels bolted together, unpacked ...	5'2" 157.5 cm.	5'2" 157.5 cm.	2'10" 86.4 cm.	7¼	368

In pursuance of this company's policy of constant development, the right is reserved to depart, without notice, from any detail illustrated or specified in this leaflet, without incurring the obligation to provide such modifications on machines previously delivered.

MARSHALL, SONS AND COMPANY, LIMITED, GAINSBOROUGH, LINCS., ENGLAND

Telephone: Gainsborough 2301   Telegrams: Marshalls, Gainsborough

Specification details for pre-production MP6

With power to spare

the Marshall M.P.6, 70 b.h.p.

THE MARSHALL M.P.6 is designed for exceptionally heavy duties which call for a tractor with power and to spare. The M.P.6 does the job faster. It saves manpower and time.

Here are features to note :

Power Leyland U/E 350 6-cylinder 4-stroke engine, developing 70 b.h.p.

Speed Range embraces 6 speeds forward ranging from 1.71 to 13 m.p.h., and 2 in reverse, operated by a single ball-mounted lever control.

Pull In excess of 9,500 lbs. in 1st speed. In excess of 7,500 lbs. in 2nd speed.

Driver Comfort Weatherproof foam-rubber seating and convenient grouping of controls reduce fatigue to the minimum.

First Class Servicing Marshall distributors ensure a complete after-sales service.

Ask your local Marshall agent for Publication 2970 or write to Marshalls* at the address below.

A copy of the N.I.A.E. Report No. BS/NIAE/5614 is available on application.

Product of the Marshall Organisation

Marshall Sons & Co. Ltd., Gainsborough, Lincs.

Introducing the Marshall MP6

Early Marshall MP6 sales brochure cover

and were not prepared to release the tractor until they were confident that all faults had been eliminated.

When the MP6 finally became available in January 1956, it had received a small number of alterations. With the exception of the strengthened final drive housing, mechanically the MP6 had received little change. Cosmetically, the panelwork and nose section were altered to allow for increased engine cooling efficiency and to provide ease of access to the radiator for periodic cleaning. To facilitate removal of the engine canopy, the air intake pipe was repositioned and this improved accessibility for repairs.

The MP6 was in a class of its own, as no other tractor in Europe could equal its size and power. Marshalls felt confident that they had produced a tractor to compete against the highly powered American tractors.

With an overall length of 12 ft 8 in and a maximum height of 7 ft 3 in, the MP6 towered above the average-sized tractor. The rugged construction of the transmission and final drive assembly provided a clear indication that this tractor had been built to endure many hours of arduous work. The 70 h.p. Leyland 6-cylinder engine boasted ample power, with its comparatively low governed maximum engine

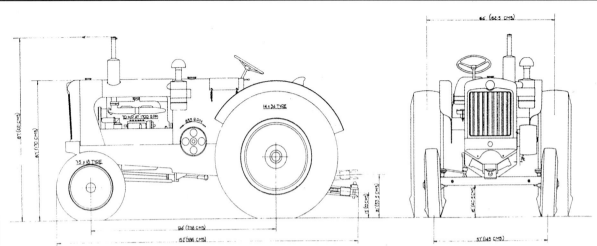

ENGINE
Leyland type UE.350. 6 cylinder. 4 stroke. 351 cu. in. (5760 c.c.) displacement. Compression Ignition Oil Engine developing 70 B.H.P. at 1700 R.P.M. Electric Starting. Engine Cooling by fan, radiator and water pump. Water cooled type, lubricating oil cooler.

CLUTCH
14" Borg & Beck dry single plate, pedal operated.

GEARBOX
6 speeds forward and 2 reverse. Single ball mounted lever control for all speeds, with separate lever for reverse.

SPEEDS AND DRAWBAR PULLS

		Speeds at Governed R.P.M.		Drawbar Pulls*	
		m.p.h.	Km./hr.	lbs.	Kgs.
Forward	1st	1·71	2,75	9800	4450
	2nd	3·00	4,83	7600	3450
	3rd	4·06	6,55	5350	2430
	4th	5·06	8,15	4050	1840
	5th	7·55	12,20	2450	1120
	6th	13·00	20,92	1150	525
Reverse	1st	3·06	4,92		
	2nd	5·32	8,57		

*The above drawbar pulls are with hydroflated 15·00—34 tyres and wheelweights on dry tarmacadam and with the exception of the sixth speed are recorded in Report of Test BS/NIAE/56/4 conducted by the N.I.A.E. For continuous heavy duty calculate upon approximately 75% of the above figures.

TYRES
Rear 14.00—34.   Front 7.50—18.

DRAWBAR
Swinging type adjustable for height. Height from ground 13"—21" (33 cm.—53,5 cm.). Width of swing 32" (81 cm.).

BRAKES
Totally enclosed, contracting bands, acting on 15"dia. drums fitted to differential shafts which have 4.93/1 ratio to rear axles. Pedals operate brakes independently or together, by connecting plate.
A hand lever applies brakes simultaneously, through compensating gear.

DIMENSIONS
Wheelbase   ... ... 94" or 114¾" 238 cm. or 290,7 cm.
Overall length ... ...152"   386 ,,
  ,,   width ... ...80½"   204 ,,
Height to top of radiator 67"   170 ,,
  ,,   ,, ,, ,, exhaust 87"   221 ,,

Wheel track, rear	...	64" or 78"	162,5 cm. or 198 cm. (variable by reversing wheels).
Wheel track, front	...	57"	145 c.m.
Ground clearance	...	16"	40,5 ,,
Weight in working order (without water ballast in tyres)	8480 lbs. approx.	3850 kg.
Weight (including water ballast)	9850 lbs. approx.	4470 kg.

OPTIONAL EXTRAS

Tyres. 15.00—34 rear tyres instead of 14.00—34.

Belt Pulley. 13⅞" dia. × 8½" face (35 cm. × 21,6 cm.), controlled by main clutch. 855 R.P.M. giving belt speed 3100 ft./min. (950 metres/min.).

Power Take-off. 1¾" dia (4,45 cm.) 6 spline shaft. Clockwise from rear. 29½" (75 cm.) from ground, 1⅛" (2,85 cm.) to right of tractor centre line, shaft end 13½" (34 cm.) forward of drawbar hitch pin. Speed 544 R.P.M. with engine at 1700 R.P.M.

Wheel Weights.

	Total Weight added	
1 inner disc per wheel	240 lbs.	100 kg.
1 inner and 1 outer disc per wheel	600 lbs.	270 kg.
1 inner, 1 outer and 1 middle disc per wheel	1000 lbs.	450 kg.
1 inner, 1 outer and 2 middle discs per wheel	1400 lbs.	635 kg.
1 inner, 1 outer and 3 middle discs per wheel	1800 lbs.	800 kg.

ELECTRIC LIGHTS
12 volt lighting sets for road and/or field work.

APPROXIMATE SHIPPING SPECIFICATION

	Length		Breadth		Height		Cwts.	Kgs.
Fully packed Main case ...11' 5"	348 cm.	6' 9"	206 cm.	5' 2"	158 cm.	84	4267
Also one Pair hind wheels bolted together unpacked... 5' 2"	158 cm.	5' 2"	158 cm.	2' 10"	86 cm.	7¼	368
Top boxed on Wheels ... 12' 3"	373 cm.	6' 4"	193 cm.	5' 11"	180 cm.	74	3759
Protected on Wheels ... 12' 3"	373 cm.	6' 4"	193 cm.	6' 4"	193 cm.	71	3607

In pursuance of this company's policy of constant development, the right is reserved to depart, without notice, from any detail illustrated or specified in this leaflet, without incurring the obligation to provide such modifications on machines previously delivered

MARSHALL SONS AND COMPANY LIMITED, GAINSBOROUGH, LINCS., ENGLAND

Telephone: Gainsborough 2301   Telegrams: Marshalls, Gainsborough

Specification details for production MP6

Marshall MP6 at work in Royston, Bedfordshire in 1957

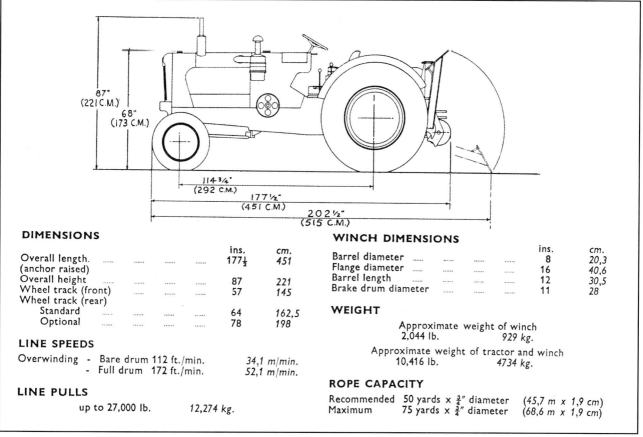

DIMENSIONS

				ins.	cm.
Overall length. (anchor raised)				177½	451
Overall height				87	221
Wheel track (front)				57	145
Wheel track (rear)					
Standard				64	162,5
Optional				78	198

LINE SPEEDS

Overwinding - Bare drum 112 ft./min.   *34,1 m/min.*
 - Full drum 172 ft./min.   *52,1 m/min.*

LINE PULLS

up to 27,000 lb.   *12,274 kg.*

WINCH DIMENSIONS

				ins.	cm.
Barrel diameter				8	20,3
Flange diameter				16	40,6
Barrel length				12	30,5
Brake drum diameter				11	28

WEIGHT

Approximate weight of winch
2,044 lb.   *929 kg.*

Approximate weight of tractor and winch
10,416 lb.   *4734 kg.*

ROPE CAPACITY

Recommended 50 yards x ¾" diameter *(45,7 m x 1,9 cm)*
Maximum   75 yards x ¾" diameter *(68,6 m x 1,9 cm)*

Long wheel base version of MP6 with Boughton winch

speed of 1700 r.p.m.

A long wheel based version of the MP6 was available specifically for industrial applications. Lengthening the tractor had easily been accomplished by reversing the final drive housing and extending the overall length to 16 ft 10½ in. The long wheel based version was usually recommended for added stability if the tractor was to be equipped with heavy ancillary equipment.

A purpose-built long wheel based forestry MP6 was introduced at the 1958 Royal Show. The tractor on display received a Boughton series 2 single-speed winch, which incorporated a swivel headed fair lead. The winch featured a reversible drum and was provided with a standard length of 50 yd of ¾ in wire rope. An option of 75 yd of rope could be installed upon request.

The winch was capable of producing a mean line pull of 27,000 lb and therefore capable of accomplishing most duties required in timber extraction. A heavy duty front bumper and nose guard, which provided adequate protection against damage, were essential when the tractor was working amongst heavy undergrowth.

The additional weight of the winch and fittings increased the tractor's weight considerably. A basic tractor was indeed heavy enough, weighing in at 8480 lb, and when the winch and fittings were added, it topped the scales at a staggering 10,416 lb.

Marshalls offered a wide range of accessories for the MP6 to cater for various duties. These additional features included 15 in x 34 in rear tyres to replace the standard 14 in x 34 in, a belt pulley and a centrally mounted power take-off shaft. Rear wheel weights ranging from 240 to 1800 lb were available to enhance traction. The weights consisted of separate cast iron sections which attached to the outer face of the rear wheel. The provision of a 12 volt lighting set provided ample power for working late at night, and the set comprised two head lamps, side lights, tail light and the option of a rear mounted work light.

Marshalls were always willing to oblige when customers requested their additions to specification and tractors were tailored to suit. This accounts

MP6 with Boughton winch hauling timber

Long wheel base MP6 complete with Boughton heavy duty winch and front bumper bar

Long wheel base MP6 with Cookes heavy duty winch

Demonstration MP6 tractor serial no. 6520002 fitted with giant low pressure rear tyres hauling two 6-furrow ploughs at Royston in Bedfordshire 1957

MP6 crated for export (note the wheel weights bolted to the side of the tractor)

MP6 with 20-furrow disc plough in Australia

Typical load for the MP6: six trailers loaded with sugar cane in the West Indies
(Rural History Centre, University of Reading)

for a number of tractors, listed in the erection books, that left the works with a variety of accessories such as air compressors, hydraulic pumps, foot throttles and even an air braking system.

When the MP6 finally became available in 1956 it had encountered a price increase of £50, which was due to a rise in costs of manufacturing materials. An MP6 in basic specification retailed at £1450, a price far out of reach for the average farmer. The MP6 was too big and cumbersome to suit the average British farm and not surprisingly sales were low in the home market. Marshalls were not deterred by this lack of response, for the simple reason that the MP6 had been primarily designed and targeted to be exported.

The three prototypes received the serial nos. 6520001, 6520002 and 6520003. Those produced thereafter commenced production with serial no. 6740001 and followed through in succession.

The first batch were exported to prime areas, with Australia receiving the first consignment of eight tractors produced. Export orders began to flourish due to a strong marketing strategy. Orders for the MP6 increased steadily with great demand from satisfied customers filtering through from France, Spain, Africa, Australia and the West Indies. The MP6 excelled in heavy cultivation and also gained an excellent reputation for hauling. It was widely used in Australia and the West Indies for pulling trailers loaded with sugar cane from the fields to the processing plant. Sales on the home market remained unchanged.

Many of Marshalls' main distributors in Britain lodged complaints concerning the lack of a rear mounted 3-point linkage system. They were adamant that the tractor would have received far more interest if such a device had been introduced. Marshalls continued to insist that fitting 3-point linkage to the MP6 was unnecessary, for the simple reason that no one at that time had manufactured a suitably mounted implement to cater for a tractor above 50 h.p.

Although export orders continued to show promise, there was an increasing presence of American tractors in areas where the MP6 had established a foothold. The two year delay in availability of the MP6 had allowed rival American companies to improve and develop their high horsepower tractors. Marshalls could not compete against their low prices, as they simply did not have the facilities or manpower to equal the American competition in mass production.

Front cover from later sales brochure for MP6 tractor

The year 1958 was one of disruption for the MP6. Once again Marshalls were forced to increase their prices. Reoccurring difficulties with the final drive gears and troublesome starting with the Leyland engine did little to encourage customer confidence, and resulted in a further deterioration of sales. A number of Marshall agents reported that they were experiencing difficulty in selling the MP6 and could no longer afford to keep such an expensive piece of equipment in stock. The infiltration of American tractors into Canada had made the MP6 totally unmarketable. The only remedy that Marshalls were prepared to offer was to reallocate tractors to areas that had been least affected by the lack of demand. By 1960, Marshalls recognised they could do little to encourage customer loyalty and admitted defeat by withdrawing the MP6 from the market.

The last MP6 serial no. 6740194 left Britannia Works on 7 December 1961 and was distributed through agents Corey Brothers to Algiers. Sales figures clearly reflect the lack of demand for the MP6, as throughout the total period of production only 197 tractors were manufactured.

Marshalls did not continue with the production of wheeled tractors or re-enter the wheeled tractor market until almost 25 years later, when they launched the Marshall 100 tractor in 1984, fitted with a Leyland 6-cylinder engine.

Looking back at the performance figures of the MP6 and at such a size for a British tractor in the late 1950s, many people and even Marshalls have voiced the suggestion that it was developed too early for the British farmer. The country was not ready for such a large tractor at that time! If the MP6 had been launched in the late sixties or early seventies, with 3-point linkage and power steering, it might have been well accepted.

MP6 WORLDWIDE DISTRIBUTION

197 tractors were made and sold in the following countries:

France		37	South Africa	8
Australia		33	Syria	5
Western Australia	22		Tanganyika	3
Queensland	4		Greece	2
New South Wales	3		Portugal	1
Southern Australia	3		Russia	1
Victoria	1		Iran	1
West Indies		31	Iraq	1
Spain		24	Nigeria	1
Algeria		19	British Guiana	1
Rhodesia		18	Southern Ireland	1
Great Britain		10	Total	197

Fowler Challenger Mark I with Marshall ED5 engine (P Gaskins)

Marshall MP6 complete with full lighting set, hydraulic power take-off and full set of rear wheel weights

Marshall MP6 in its long wheel based form

Marshall MP6 in regular use in Australia in 1988   (S Donetta)

Marshall MP6 in regular use in Victoria, Australia in 1989   (S Donetta)

CHAPTER 9

Tracks and Rails

FOWLER VF CRAWLER

Following successful demonstrations in 1948, the VF received a very positive response, with the media extolling the virtues of its simplicity of design, high power output and low fuel consumption.

The introductory price of £1060 was indeed competitive in relation to the few other diesel crawler tractors on the market. Although the VF did not boast a smooth-running multi-cylinder engine, it had an engine that had already proved its capabilities in the Field Marshall wheeled tractor. The 6-speed gearbox provided a wide range of working speeds needed for a medium range crawler tractor. The main feature of the VF was the introduction of balanced power steering.

This enabled the driver to steer in either direction and maintain equal power on both tracks without reducing the engine's performance. This action was achieved by the introduction of a patented, controlled epicyclic differential. When an individual brake was applied it activated a compound train of gears, which immediately reduced the speed of one sprocket and simultaneously increased that of the other.

Another exclusive feature was the introduction of a track stabiliser, which consisted of a patented cranked front axle. The cranked action enabled each track to operate as an independent unit and eliminated the tendency to track toe in and out.

Prototype Fowler VF crawler June 1947

Rear view of prototype VF crawler (note the Field Marshall style rear platform)

Second prototype VF undergoing field test work in 1947. The flat throttle knob and steering box mounting bracket display the typical use of Field Marshall components

A dry-fibred multi-plate clutch replaced the cone clutch used in the Field Marshall wheeled tractors. This multi-plate proved advantageous, with its increased face contact, and lessened the possibility of slippage when engaged upon constant heavy loads. Except for marginally different gear ratios, the transmission layout was of the same principle as that of the Field Marshall series 3, described in Chapter 6.

The engine was subjected to very little alteration and retained the characteristics of those that powered the wheeled tractors. One minor change was the direction of rotation to

clockwise, which allowed for an additional shaft in the final drive reduction. A Vokes air pre-cleaner became a standard feature in tractors until September 1949. Thereafter the Vokes part was replaced by the Burgess dome shaped pre-cleaner, which was favoured over the former for its ease of maintenance. Pre-cleaners were essential on crawler tractors due to their tendency to create dust bowls, thrown up from the track plates.

An initial decision to market the new crawler as the Fowler Marshall VF was withdrawn at an early stage. Early sales literature depicted the Marshall baton, affixed to the tractor's centre

(Text continues on p.176)

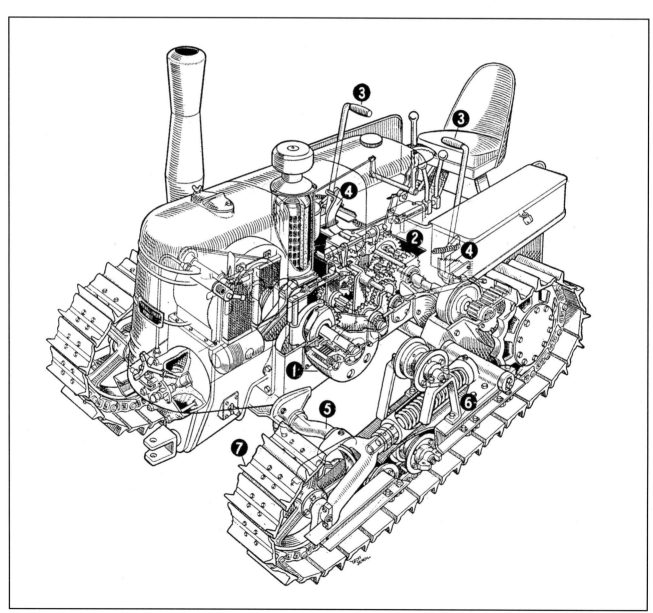

Early Fowler VF crawler 1948 model (bucket seat)

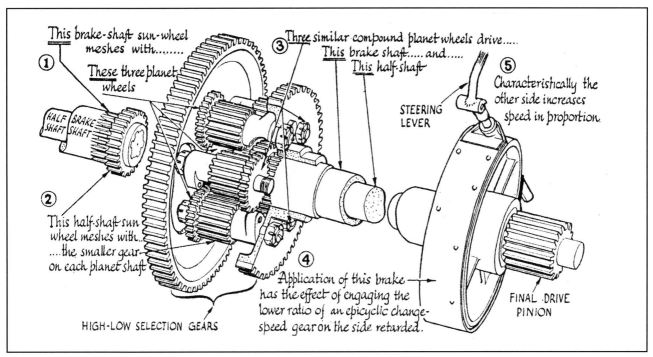

① This brake-shaft sun-wheel meshes with........

These three planet wheels

HALF SHAFT BRAKE SHAFT

② This half-shaft sun wheel meshes with.. ....the smaller gear on each planet shaft

HIGH-LOW SELECTION GEARS

③ Three similar compound planet wheels drive..... This brake shaft..... and..... This half-shaft

④ Application of this brake has the effect of engaging the lower ratio of an epicyclic change-speed gear on the side retarded.

⑤ Characteristically the other side increases speed in proportion.

STEERING LEVER

FINAL DRIVE PINION

Illustrated working of the balance power steering employed in the Fowler VF

Worm's view of an early VF ploughing

Advertising sales photos of VF (note the Fowler Marshall baton affixed to the centre bonnet)

"That must have been the Mark V F"

FOUR FURROWS, cut through heavy loam to a width of 11 in. and a depth of 8 in. — a typical achievement of the new Fowler Diesel Crawler Mark V F.

Thorough tests have shown that the Mark V F can also steadily and continuously pull: *a 2-furrow deep-digger plough*, set to a width of 17 in. and a depth of 14 in. working in clay: or *a 13-tine Cultivator*, set to a depth of 6 in. and working in heavy loam.

Price £1060 ex Works. Write for Illustrated Brochure to John Fowler & Co. (Leeds) Ltd., Leeds, 10. Tel. Leeds 30731 or get in touch with your Local Distributor. No W.A.E.C. permits now necessary.

THIS ALL-BRITISH Crawler Tractor embodies the following features : 40-*h.p.* at belt, at 750 r.p.m. with corresponding drawbar pull, according to conditions ; *fuel consumption*, under normal conditions, a gallon of Diesel fuel to an hour's ploughing: *Single-Cylinder, two-stroke Diesel engine :* this power unit, already tried and proved in the famous Field-Marshall tractors has only three prime moving parts . . . *Track stabiliser*, exclusive to the Mark V F, eliminating destructive "toe-in" and "toe-out", but allowing free oscillating over rough ground ; *power delivered at all times equally to both tracks* thus giving smooth and exceptional manœuvrability. Extremely low centre of gravity giving high stability on steep ground.

THE FOWLER MARK V F
BRITISH DIESEL CRAWLER

A PRODUCT OF THE MARSHALL ORGANIZATION

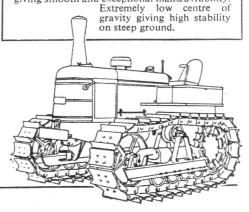

Publicity for Fowler VF crawler December 1948

bonnet, heralding the Marshall and Fowler emblem. Before full production commenced, credit was passed over to Fowlers to establish sectional marketing. Marshalls concentrated on the production of wheeled tractors, combine harvesters, threshing machines and road rollers, whilst Fowlers focused on the specialised market in the production of crawler tractors, which in time ranged from 40 to 150 h.p.

The VF was in its development stage in early 1947. Due to lengthy test periods, full production did not commence until March 1948. The first tractor received the serial no. 4700001 and others followed on in succession. A small number of early tractors were painted the bright Fowler orange but this colour was discontinued in favour of the Field Marshall's mid Brunswick green.

Extras were extremely limited, a 12 volt lighting set being the only one. Gradually a wider range of equipment became available as the popularity of the VF flourished. The most successful and welcome addition to the civil

engineering was the bulldozer blade attachment. Customers were offered a variety of units, those manufactured by Bray and Blaw Knox being amongst the most popular.

Bray were the first to offer their fully hydraulically operated bulldozer with any success. Introduced in 1948, the Bray unit offered the facility of angle dozing, which was simply effected by the repositioning of two locking pins. The drive to the hydraulic pump was taken via an angle drive from the first motion shaft of the gearbox. When the clutch was disengaged, the drive to the hydraulic pump would cease and inconveniently isolate operation of the bulldozer blade.

Blaw Knox of Kensington, London, introduced their bulldozer to fit the VF in early 1949. Their attachment was similar in build to the sturdily constructed Bray, but featured a smaller blade. The hydraulic pump was driven directly from the outer face of the clutch pulley via a chain and sprocket. This provided a live drive, which

Early produced VF finished in Fowler colours circa 1948

The first Bray bulldozer fitted to a VF crawler circa 1948
(Rural History Centre, University of Reading)

allowed the driver to have full control over tractor and bulldozer, thus enabling the driver to change gear without losing drive to the hydraulics. Despite the added advantage of Blaw Knox's live drive, the Bray bulldozer appeared to be the more popular of the two, mainly because of the larger blade surface.

Bomford offered their Sapper bulldozer attachments for use with the VF crawler. The Sapper Minor consisted of a manually operated hydraulic pump for lifting and lowering the blade. Operation of this particular bulldozer was slow and indeed strenuous, which resulted in the lack of demand. The Sapper Major was provided with a hydraulic pump, driven by a belt from the engine's flywheel. The blade could be raised in the conventional way, by a lever-operated spool valve. Sales for this also proved rather disappointing. Both of these attachments were unsuitable for continual heavy work, due to their light construction, which accounted for their unpopularity.

Tractors sent overseas were often equipped with bulldozers manufactured within the country of export. Australia and New Zealand offered a

Publicity advertisement for VF crawler 1949

VF with Blaw Knox bulldozer
(Rural History Centre, University of Reading)

Bomford Sapper Major bulldozer in use on Fowler VF crawler
(Rural History Centre, University of Reading)

Fowler VF crawler and Field Marshall series 2 tractors at the Paris Show in 1949 (J Barbier)

Marshall and Fowler tractors at the Royal Smithfield Show, Earls Court, London in December 1949

wide and varied source of bulldozer attachments, built in their homeland by companies such as Brown, Malcolm Moore, Vengar and Frieghter.

Street plates, extra deep spuds and the option of track plates 16 in wide were introduced as ancillary items in 1948. The wider track plates proved popular in the flat wet areas of Britain, where there was a recognised need to reduce ground pressure and increase traction.

Fowlers focused upon the timber industry and offered their sturdy self-contained winch, which provided the operator with an increased range of abilities and proved adequately capable of exerting a mean line pull of 12,000 lb. Specifically designed for the Fowler VF, the winch was conveniently placed beneath the driver's platform. For ease of operation a free-rolling drum was incorporated, provided with 75 yd of $^3/_4$ in wire rope and a retractable speed of 94 ft per minute. The drive to the winch was supplied via a bevel drive unit, from the first motion shaft in the gearbox. A duplex chain conveyed the drive through to the winch drum and brake assembly.

Difficulties arose when customers specified the provision of both the Fowler winch and the Bray bulldozer attachment, as they both relied upon the first motion shaft for power take-off. The problem was rectified in later years with the introduction of a special drive unit which enabled the winch and bulldozer to share the same drive shaft.

Sales of the Fowler winch proved rather disappointing. Customers often complained that the rope retraction speed was too fast. Frequently, a snatch block had to be used in line to reduce the speed and maintain an even pull. Although the provision of a winch was an uncommon feature on a crawler tractor, Fowlers recognised that they had to offer an alternative if their own unit did not satisfy customers' needs. More often customers specified their preference, which accounted for many tractors receiving the popular Boughton winch.

Despite the unpopularity of the Fowler winch, in 1949 Fowlers introduced a purpose-built version VF specifically for timber extraction, which featured wide track plates and a front bumper bar. This particular winch was little favoured by customers; hence only a limited number were produced. The majority of agricultural tractors received the power take-off shaft attachment, due to the increasing popularity of power-driven implements. This drive unit was mounted to the left-hand side of the gearbox and also utilised the drive from the first motion shaft. A further option of a centrally mounted power take-off shaft could be provided for those who preferred a central drive. This simply utilised the

VF with heavy duty Fowler winch and front bumper bar extracting timber
(Rural History Centre, University of Reading)

A rare and unusual combination of Fowler winch and Bray bulldozer. A special drive arrangement had to be installed to provide the power for both pieces of equipment. Both winch and bulldozer take their drive from the first motion shaft in the gearbox

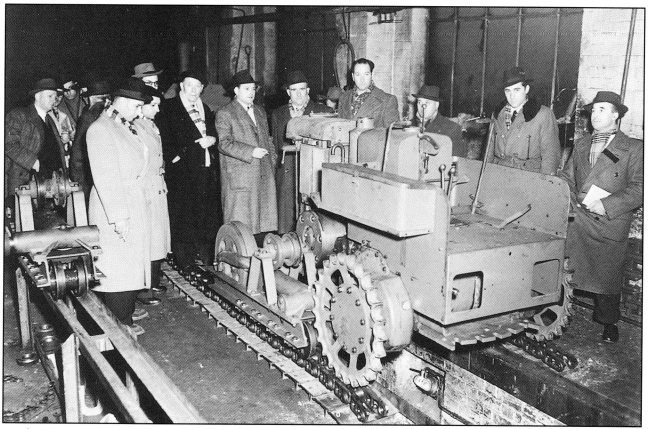

Fowler VF assembly at Leeds in 1950   (Rural History Centre, University of Reading)

VF crawlers undergoing dynamometer testing at Leeds

VF with centrally mounted power take-off, powering a Howard rotavator
(Rural History Centre, University of Reading)

Fowler VF installed with an auxiliary hydraulic pump to power a la Plante-Choate scraper at work in Ashford, Kent in 1952 (Rural History Centre, University of Reading)

drive from the side mounted unit via a sprocket and chain, then continued to rotate in a clockwise direction. This provided the prerequisite speed of 550 r.p.m. which was required for the majority of power-driven farm implements.

Driver comfort was not always considered of importance to a farm tractor. Most operators were left to face the elements and often devised their own form of protection against atmospheric conditions. However, Portland seized the opportunity to bridge this hole in the market and upon request produced a metal framed all-weather cab. Though this proffered adequate protection, the vibration generated through the flimsy panelwork often proved so unbearable that more often than not it was removed.

The VF encountered many changes throughout production. Many of these improvements and alterations simply filtered through as a result of the continued development of the Field Marshall tractor. One area which received regular modifications was the track frame and running gear. In

1948 the spoked front idlers were superseded by heavy cast idlers to add extra ballast to the front end. Following this, tractors produced after serial no. 4700961 received a bench seat to replace the former bucket seat. The bench seat offered a safer working area and also enhanced driver comfort.

Since the undercarriage of the crawler had a tendency to experience a certain amount of damage, the introduction of a belly pan was a welcome addition as this afforded protection to the underside of the engine. As a result of reoccurring failures with the cast iron front idlers yokes, tractors manufactured after serial no. 4704086 received cast steel yokes. Tractors that had been fitted with the heavy cast front idlers encountered problems caused by the additional weight. The final drive housing also received attention, as there were repeated problems with hairline fractures which appeared in the final drive casing. These cracks allowed oil to escape, gradually draining the housings, which resulted in serious damage to the bearings, drive shafts

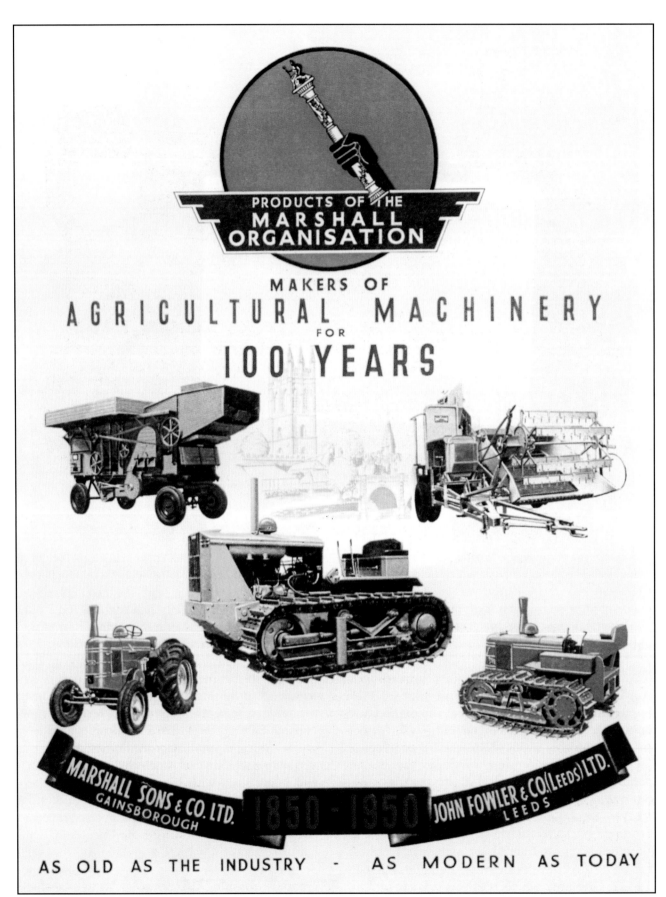

Advert marking the Marshall Fowler centenary

KEY TO NUMBERS ON DRAWING

1. 40-h.p. single cylinder 2-stroke diesel engine.
2. Fuel injector.
3. Compression release valve.
4. Hand-start valve.
5. Ignition paper holder.
6. Cartridge starter.
7. Radiator.
8. Oil filter.
9. Oil filler cap.
10. Front drawbar.
11. Fuel filter.
12. Air cleaner.
13. Clutch and belt pulley.
14. Clutch brake pad.
15. Clutch operating fork.
16. First motion shaft.
17. Second motion shaft.
18. Power take-off.
18b. Power take-off control lever.
19. 3-speed change-gear lever.
20. High-low change-gear lever.
21. Governor control.
22. Clutch hand control.
23. Clutch foot control.
24. Steerage unit.
25. L.H. steerage band.
26. Tool box.
27. Final drive.
28. Track recoil spring.
29. Track tension adjustment.
30. Oil pipe to L.H. main crankshaft bearing.
31. Engine and transmission undershield.
32. Torsional front axle.
33. Rear cross beam.
34. Steering levers.
35. Swinging drawbar.

Fowler VF crawler 1949 model (bench seat)

and corresponding gears. The problem seemed to be more particular to those tractors fitted with bulldozer blades, as these machines were constantly worked at full capacity. Upon investigation, the cause of the weakness was traced to the half shaft and sprocket flexing. This action could not be absorbed by the casting and inevitably fractured. However, by fitting a ¼ in steel diaphragm spacer between the final drive casing and gearbox the problem was greatly reduced, since the spacer helped to absorb any additional movement thus preventing further damage. Starting from tractor no. 4703785, all machines received the diaphragm plate and as time bore witness to its success, the diaphragm plate became available as a listed part to fit existing tractors.

All these improvements to the VF were reflected in a weighty price increase. Despite the £200 increase to £1260 in 1949, the VF remained popular and compared favourably with its main competitors, Caterpillar, David Brown, County of Fleet, Hampshire, and International. Again, it was the simplicity and economic values of the VF that were in its favour.

The business association of Marshall and Fowler created ideal opportunities to distribute the VF into areas where the Field Marshall had already become well established. Indeed, there were world-wide markets where the Field Marshall had become the brand leader and had gained a substantial control of the market. Customers, both at home and abroad, needed little introduction to the economic benefits of the single-cylinder diesel engine, and sales figures reflected this. Overseas orders reached a high point in 1951 with an order from the Indian Government for over a hundred crawlers to aid in the construction of the Bhakra Dam. France, Spain, Canada, Africa, New Zealand and Australia also continued to place large orders for the VF.

Part of the fleet of over 100 Fowler VF bulldozers employed in building the Bhakra Dam in India

Fowler FD3 crawler tractor

A 1951 Fowler VF crawler, fitted with 16 in wide track plates

Fowler 40 h.p. narrow gauge locomotive, fitted with Marshall single-cylinder diesel engine

FOWLER NARROW GAUGE LOCOMOTIVE

Suitably impressed by the simplicity and performance of the VF crawler, Fowlers introduced the Marshall single-cylinder engine to their range of narrow gauge industrial railway locomotives. Making its first public appearance at the British Industries Fair, held at Birmingham in April 1949, the new locomotive boasted all the economic values and ruggedness provided by the single-cylinder engine. It was targeted for market distribution to Third World countries, which would benefit from its design and operation.

The engine was built to the same specification as that of the VF crawler, the only major difference being that the clutch pulley assembly was removed and was replaced with a large counter balance flywheel. The power from the engine to the gearbox was transmitted via a heavy duplex chain. The gearbox was of simple construction and provided three forward and three reverse speeds, transmitted through two cone clutches. These were activated by a simple single lever action to determine the direction of travel. Drive to the axles, from the gearbox, was also by duplex chains. The axles were secured to the chassis by large laminated springs which reduced the vibration generated by the momentum of the single-cylinder engine.

The locomotive was made available in variable gauges, ranging from 1 ft 11¾ in to 3ft 6 in. Braking was implemented by means of a single screw lever, which, when applied, caused two large friction pads to make contact with the front axle only. The height to the top of the canopy was 8 ft 8 in and the overall length was 10 ft 1 in. A fully enclosed driver's cab was available as opposed to the four post corrugated sheet canopy, which was a standard fixture. The whole outfit was of typical solid and robust Marshall Fowler construction and tipped the scales in working order at 7 tons 5 cwt. Performance figures appeared encouraging, assuming a track rolling resistance of 20 lb per ton in first gear, and 10 lb in second and third. The locomotive was capable of hauling a load of 125 tons in top gear on the level; 17 tons up a gradient of 1:50 and 6 tons up 1:25. The corresponding figures for the work in first gear were 190 tons on the level, 53 tons up a gradient of 1:50 and 28 up 1:25.

Several problems, however, prevented the locomotive's success. The tendency to leave the rails at high speed, coupled with uncontrollable vibration, did little to grace its credibility and encourage custom. As a result, only 46 units were manufactured, with only three of these being housed in Britain. The remaining 43 were distributed to Bulgaria, Africa, India and South America. Production ceased due to a continual decline in orders, and the locomotive was finally discontinued in 1952.

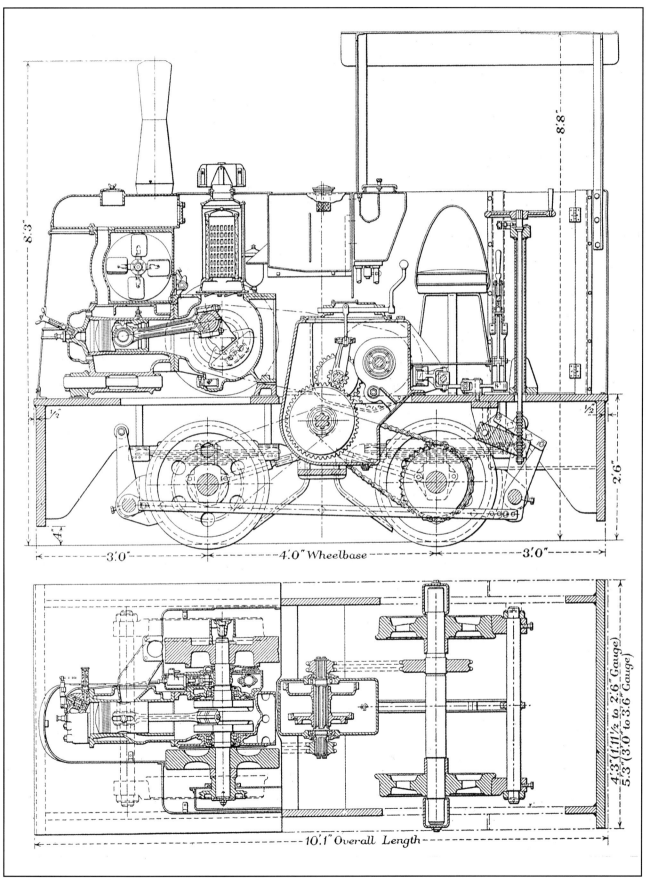

Fowler single cylinder 40 h.p. narrow gauge rail locomotive

Fowler single-cylinder diesel locomotive

CHAPTER 10
A Time for Change

In October 1952, commencing with serial no. 4704659, the VF progressed into the VFA. The engine's performance had been improved upon and incorporated many of the uprated components featured in the Field Marshall series 3A tractor. After serial no. 4704953, the VFA received the pressurised cooling system. The fuel filtration system was also changed to incorporate twin fuel filters, again a feature of the Field Marshall series 3 and 3A. The track frame and final drive assemblies continued to be improved upon. They were strengthened and equipped with fixing points where a bulldozer blade could be attached. Continual problems with the final drive housings necessitated further modifications, which were effected by late 1952. A redesigned and strengthened drive casing, half shaft and hub assembly was later introduced, after serial no. 4705121. Whilst the first batch of approximately 300 VFAs were finished in the familiar mid Brunswick green, thereafter the colour became bright orange, following the trend set by the Field Marshall series 3A.

Unfortunately the VFA could not hold its own against the competitive market, despite the increased pulling power to 11,200 lb. By 1953 demand had tailed off somewhat dramatically, and Fowlers sales team recognised that its unpopularity lay with the single-cylinder engine. Though this offered simplicity of design and economic advantages, when it came to power, the VFA was at a disadvantage. On the market at this

Fowler VFA with Portland cab circa 1953

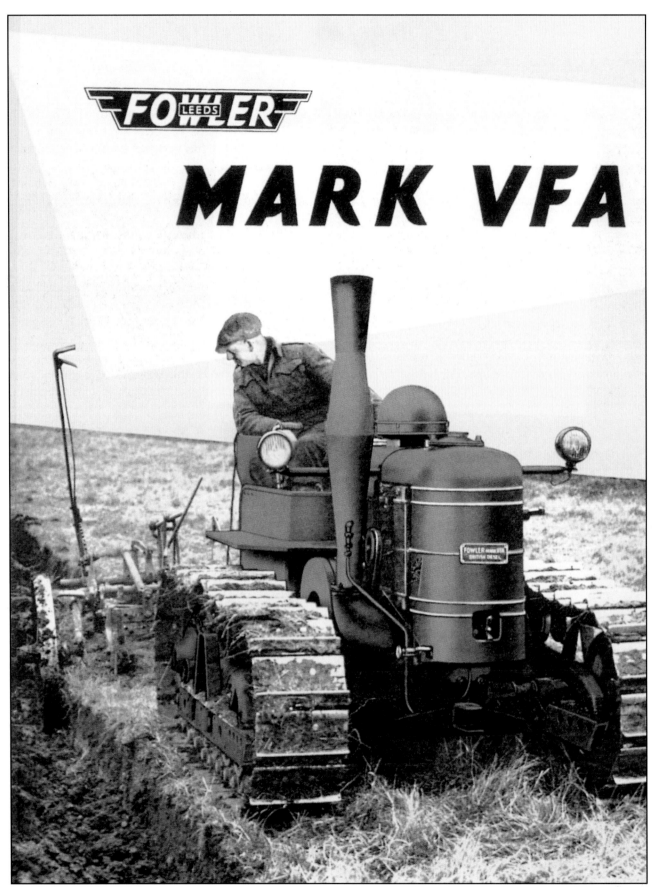

Fowler VFA crawler advert

Crown Estates Windsor taking delivery of a new VFA in February 1954
(Rural History Centre, University of Reading)

Fowler VFA engaged upon cultivation of Windsor Park in April 1954 (note the famous Long Walk to the left)

time were new improved models by International and County, which offered greater comfort, power and a competitive price. The VFA was outdated before it could maintain a foothold in the marketplace. Marshall and Fowler mutually agreed that the single-cylinder engine either had to undergo radical changes or be replaced. As demand for the Field Marshall series 3A had also fallen, it was confirmed that the days of the single-cylinder engine were numbered.

Marshalls and Fowlers were thus forced to design new machines, a crawler to substitute for the Fowler VFA and a wheeled tractor to replace the Field Marshall. The majority of design and preparation work was carried out at the Marshall premises. Meanwhile Fowlers concentrated on the development of their Challenger crawler range, their interests in railway locomotives and the on-line production of the VFA.

Since time was of the essence, diesel engines were bought in. Perkins, Meadows, Leyland and Gardener were but a few companies that specialised in the production of multi-cylinder diesel engines. Feasibility studies were carried out on a number of engines by both Marshall and Fowler design engineers. The new prototype wheeled tractor, provisionally called the MP4, was needed to produce more power than that required for the new crawler. A Meadows 4DC330 4-cylinder diesel engine level with 65 h.p. was initially chosen for the MP4, whilst the Perkins 48 h.p. L4 engine was contracted for the new crawler. Provisionally called the Mark VII, the new crawler offered enhanced power and all the advantages associated with a 4-cylinder diesel engine. Perkins were well established and had achieved notable success in the provision of diesel engined conversion units, which had replaced the existing petrol/paraffin tractors.

Although the majority of the development and assembly work of the prototype crawler was carried out at Britannia Works, full production was allocated to the Fowler factory, where there were superior facilities to manufacture crawlers. From that time its name changed from the Mark VII to the Track Marshall. As a matter of course, the first Track Marshall underwent the normal stringent test procedures prior to its official release. A full lighting set was installed to enable test work to continue throughout the night, as it was required to work a full two weeks, day and night, stopping

Fowler VFA with Bray bulldozer fitted and coal shovel blade

Prototype Track Marshall being assembled at Britannia Works (note the tractors in the background, which are not Field Marshall 3A tractors. Closer inspection will reveal that they are VFA crawlers receiving wheeled tractor front axles)
(Rural History Centre, University of Reading)

only for refuelling and general checks.

While the prototype was tested a second Track Marshall was prepared for its debut on the market. At the Royal Show, staged in Nottingham in 1954, it received a great deal of interest which was substantiated by the number of orders taken during the week-long event. After its success at the show, the second Track Marshall went on demonstration tours throughout Britain. As it often outperformed seasoned competitors in both output and operation, these trials were a major coup for the Marshall sales team.

Before full production was handed over to Fowlers, a third Track Marshall was erected at Britannia Works. To make way for the new Track Marshall production line, VFA production was transferred from Leeds to Gainsborough, where the VFA remained until its demise in January 1957. The VFAs were assembled alongside the Field Marshall 3As and were equipped with wheeled tractor front axles, rear wheels and a temporary steering arrangement which enabled

the tractor to be driven to the Trent Works test beds. After testing, they then received the tracks and running gear. There was little demand for the VFA in Britain, and the majority were exported to countries where sales continued to show confidence; Australia, France, Spain and Canada were the main recipients.

Unfortunately, production figures are not available for either the VF or VFA crawlers. The VF commenced life at serial no. 4700001 and ended at 4704658, after which it became the VFA. This clearly shows that 4657 VF crawlers were produced between April 1948 and September 1952. It is difficult to give accurate production figures of the VFA, since the last serial number was never recorded. The VFA was reputed to have ended at around 4706000, which would account for no more than 2000 machines. Since a recently recorded world-wide register of VFA crawlers was unable to produce any evidence of tractors manufactured above the number 4706000, it seems therefore that 2000 is nearer the mark.

Prototype 48 h.p. Track Marshall undergoing field tests at the disused Skellingthorpe airfield nr. Lincoln in 1954

Second prototype 48 h.p. Track Marshall making its first appearance at the Royal Show, Nottingham in 1954
(Rural History Centre, University of Reading)

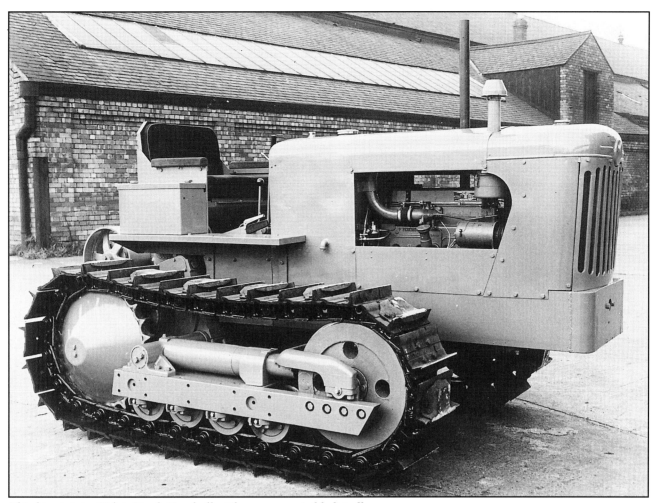

Third prototype 48 b.p. Track Marshall with rear mounted belt pulley

Very late example of a Fowler VFA crawler   (J Bloom)

CHAPTER 11
The Track Marshall

The Track Marshall was officially released in January 1956 and featured a number of alterations that had not been evident in the prototypes. Apart from the engine, the transmission of the Track Marshall was of similar arrangement to that employed in the Fowler VFA crawler. Due to the increase in power the 48 h.p. Perkins engine gave, many of the components underwent substantial strengthening and were not interchangeable with the VFA. Whilst the tracks and running gear remained fundamentally the same, it was necessary to strengthen the track frame by making it of solid steel as opposed to the previously used channel iron section. Marshalls also reinstated the track carrying rollers that had been used on the VFA but not on the prototypes.

The re-styled front bonnet and engine panelwork of the MP6 were incorporated into the Track Marshall and remained the same for 12 years. There was also an improvement to the layout of the operating controls and the driver had easier access from the comfort of a new, heavily cushioned seat. A redesigned gear selector unit simplified the selection of the speeds, whilst the Track Marshall continued to provide six forward and two reverse speeds as per the VFA. More power was offered and was therefore capable of receiving a drawbar pull of 12,000 lb in first gear, as opposed to the VFA's pull of 11,200 lb.

The choice of the Perkins engine proved advantageous, as the Track Marshall's outstanding performance was solely due to its enhanced horsepower. Basking in this success, Perkins continued to supply Marshalls with their engines for almost 40 years.

The introductory price of £1445 for a basic machine in 1956 was favourable in the marketplace, and the Track Marshall's popularity over its competitors became increasingly evident as orders continued to rise. Extra equipment, available at an additional cost, included a wide range of attachments to suit both agricultural and industrial applications. A centrally mounted power take-off shaft and rear mounted belt pulley were made available. A fully glazed driver's cab and a full 12 volt lighting set were later added to the list of ancillary equipment for agricultural use. The standard 18 in track plates could be replaced by 16 in to allow for increased traction and lighter ground pressure.

Early production Track Marshall crawler

For industrial applications, Marshalls

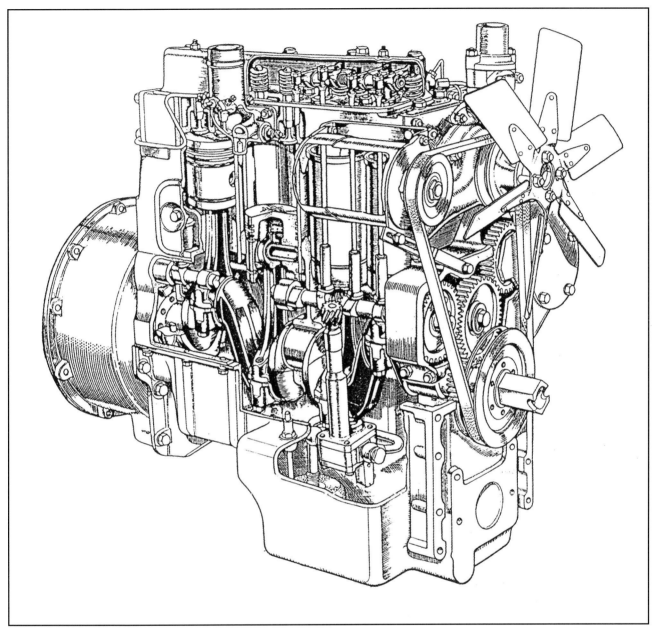

Perkins L4 diesel engine

provided their own bulldozer and single bulldozer attachment, and although Bray and Blaw Knox still offered their own units, the Marshall was priced more favourably. Fowlers did, however, cease making their own winch and contracted Boughton to manufacture a suitable unit. Boughton's HD series 2 winch was capable of a mean line pull of up to 23,000 lb. The Marshall TM2 open bowl scraper, which was primarily designed for the Fowler Challenger crawler, could be used with the Track Marshall by altering the cable control unit and using the drive from the centrally mounted power take-off shaft.

Continual development of the engine found that replacing the pneumatically controlled engine speed governor with a mechanically operated device not only gave for better control of the engine speeds but also enhanced the output by a further 2 h.p. Tractors produced after August 1956 included the mechanical governor, with sales literature proudly boasting of its improved performance at 50 h.p.

An industrial version became available in early 1957. Increased ground contact was accomplished by lengthening the track frames and adding an extra roller; this provided greater stability and was most beneficial to tractors fitted with a bulldozer blade attachment. The range of

Early 1956 production 48 h.p. Track Marshall
(Rural History Centre, University of Reading)

Early production 48 h.p. Track Marshall fitted with a full set of street plates and a Marshall bulldozer
(Rural History Centre, University of Reading)

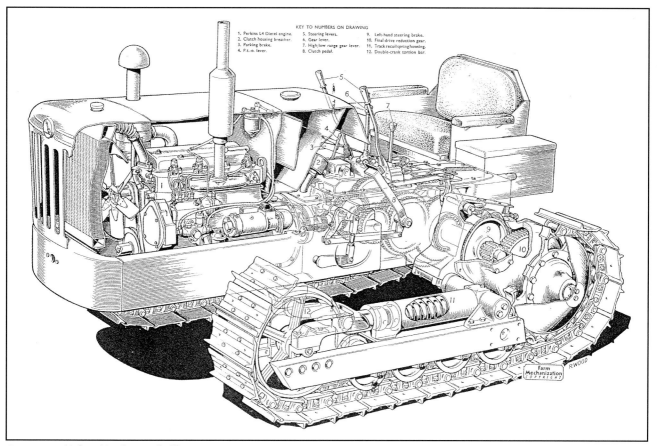

KEY TO NUMBERS ON DRAWING
1. Perkins L4 Diesel engine.   5. Steering levers.   9. Left-hand steering brake.
2. Clutch housing breather.   6. Gear lever.   10. Final drive reduction gear.
3. Parking brake.   7. High/low range gear lever. 11. Track recoil spring housing.
4. P.t.-o. lever.   8. Clutch pedal.   12. Double-crank torsion bar.

Prototype 48 h.p. Track Marshall

ancillary equipment was widened later in 1956, with the introduction of a rear mounted, hydraulically operated tool bar. This was appropriate for agricultural and industrial use and could be utilised as a ripper or sub-soiler. A hydraulic power take-off control, for powering hydraulically controlled implements, also became available around this time. A slight alteration of the track carrying roller was apparent in tractors produced after January 1957, as the roller was mounted upon a pedestal and repositioned closer to the rear drive sprocket.

The continued development of the Perkins L4 bred a new generation of engines. The L4 was replaced by a Perkins 4270D, which delivered 55 h.p. This new engine retained many of the characteristics of its forerunner, even the bore and stroke remaining unchanged. However, to obtain the 5 h.p. increase the engine speed had to be increased from 1600 to 1800 r.p.m. Timing gears replaced the conventional timing chain and the air filtration was improved by introducing a pre-cleaner bowl into the air intake stack pipe. Until production of the 55 h.p. engine, with the

exception of those machines bound for export to Australia and Canada, the Track Marshall name did not reflect its power output. From early 1959 the Track Marshall received identification as the 55, which was a brilliant marketing coup. Not only did this allow Marshalls to draw attention to the increased horsepower but also drew the buying public's attention to the machine, which was to be the first of a long-running series of ever more powerful tractors.

The year 1961 witnessed the release of the Track Marshall 70, powered by a 70 h.p. 6-cylinder Perkins engine. This fulfilled customers' needs for higher output and offered a choice of two crawler tractors, catering for both the medium and high power ends of the market. Although the Track Marshall 70 was a success, the 55 remained the market leader because of its versatility and the fact that it was the ideal size for the average British farm. By 1962 the Track Marshall 70 could be obtained with hydraulically controlled multi-plated slewing clutches, an operational facility that provided fingertip control which was more beneficial when bulldozing. The

(Text continues on p.205)

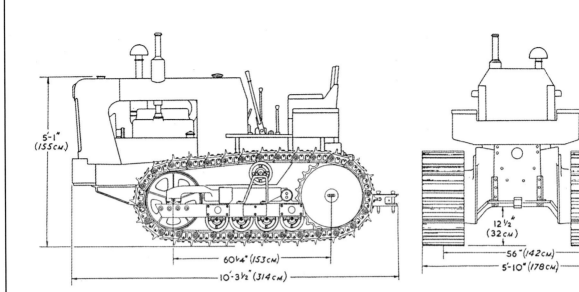

ENGINE

Perkins type L.4 diesel engine

B.H.P.	...	...	...	...	48
R.P.M.	...	...	...	...	1,600
Number of Cylinders	...	...		4	
Bore	...	...	...	4¼″	107,95 m/m
Stroke	...	...	...	4¾″	120,65 m/m
Cubic Capacity	...	...	269.5 cu. ins.	4,42 litres
Engine clutch diameter	...		14″	355,60 m/m

COOLING

By pressurised system, incorporating radiator, circulating pump and fan.

STEERING

By controlled differential, operated by hand levers.

SPEEDS AND DRAWBAR PULLS

	Speeds at Governed R.P.		M.Drawbar Pulls*	
Forward	m.p.h.	Km/hr	lbs.	Kgs
1st ...	1.31	2,10	12,100	5490
2nd ...	1.76	2,83	9,000	4085
3rd ...	2.44	3,93	6,400	2900
4th ...	2.78	4,48	5,600	2540
5th ...	3.72	5,98	3,900	1770
6th ...	5.15	8,30	2,700	1225
Reverse				
1st ...	1.01	1,63	—	—
2nd ...	2.13	3,42	—	—

* The above operating maximum drawbar pulls are recorded in Report of Test BS/NIAE/55/12 conducted by the N.I.A.E.

TRACK DIMENSIONS

Gauge, centre to centre	...	56″	142,00 cm.
Ground contact length (each track)	60¼″	153,00 cm.
Width of track plates (standard)	14″	35,56 cm.
Height of grouser	...	...	1⅞″	4,76 cm.
Track Pin diameter	...	...	1 5/16″	3,33 cm.
Track Bush diameter	...	...	2″	5,08 cm.
Track plate bolt diameter	...	9/16″	1,43 cm.
Number of rollers bottom	...	8	—
Number of rollers top	...	...	2	—
Number of plates (each side)	...	30	—
Ground contact area	...	...	1,687 sq. in.	10881 cm.²
Pull-bracing grouser area	...	521 sq. in.	3360 cm.²
Ground pressure	...	...	6.5 lb./sq. in.	458 G/cm.²
Operating weight	...	11,000 lb.	4990 Kg.

EXTRA EQUIPMENT

Provision is made for the application of the undernoted ancillary equipment:—

Central Power Take-off
Rear Mounted Belt Pulley (Driven by Power Take-off)
Heavy Duty Haulage Winch
Hydraulic Bulldozer
Hydraulic Angledozer
Driver's Cab
Electric Lighting Equipment
Street Plates
16″ (40,64 cm.) or 18″ (45,92 cm.) Track Plates
Cable Control Unit

TRACTOR DIMENSIONS

Overall length	...	...	...	123½″	314 cm.
Overall width	...	...	...	70″	178 cm.
Height to top of radiator cap	...	61″	155 cm.
Ground clearance	...	...	12½″	32 cm.

In pursuance of this company's policy of constant development, the right is reserved to depart, without notice, from any detail illustrated or specified in this leaflet, without incurring the obligation to provide such modifications on machines previously delivered.

MARSHALL, SONS AND COMPANY LIMITED, GAINSBOROUGH, LINCS., ENGLAND

Telephone: Gainsborough 2301   Telegrams: Marshalls, Gainsborough

Specification for 48 h.p. Track Marshall crawler

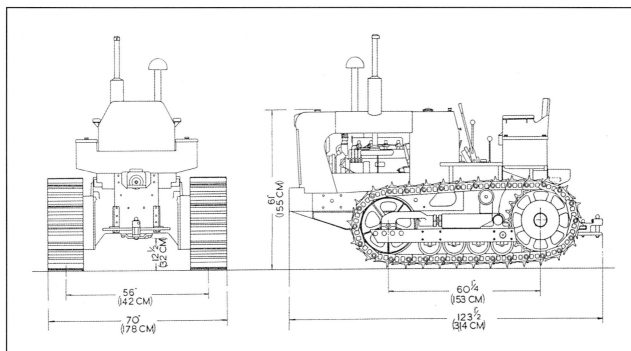

ENGINE

Perkins type L.4 diesel engine

B.H.P.	50	—
R.P.M.	1,600	—
Number of Cylinders	4	—
Bore	4¼″	107,95 mm
Stroke	4¾″	120,65 mm
Cubic Capacity	269.5 cu. ins.	4,42 litres
Engine clutch diameter	14″	355,60 mm

COOLING

By pressurised system, incorporating radiator, circulating pump and fan

STEERING

By controlled differential, operated by hand levers.

SPEEDS AND DRAWBAR PULLS

	Speeds at Governed R.P.M.		Drawbar Pulls*	
Forward	m.p.h.	Km/hr	lbs.	Kgs
1st	1.31	2,10	12,100	5490
2nd ...	1.76	2,83	9,000	4085
3rd...	2.44	3,93	6,400	2900
4th...	2.78	4,48	5,600	2540
5th...	3.72	5,98	3,900	1770
6th... ...	5.15	8,30	2,700	1225
Maximum Sustained Pull		...	13,100	5960
Reverse				
1st	1.52	2,43	—	—
2nd ...	3.22	5,15	—	—

* The above operating maximum drawbar pulls and maximum sustained pull are recorded in Report of Test BS/NIAE/55/12 conducted by the N.I.A.E.

TRACTOR DIMENSIONS

Overall length	123½″	314 cm.
Overall width	70″	178 cm.
Height to top of radiator cap...	61″	155 cm.
Ground clearance	12½″	32 cm.

TRACK DIMENSIONS

Gauge, centre to centre	...	56″	...	142,00 cm.
Ground contact length (each track) ...	...	60¼″	...	153,00 cm.
Width of track plates (standard)	...	14″	...	35,56 cm.
Height of grouser ...	...	1⅞″	...	4,76 cm.
Track Pin diameter ...	...	1⁵⁄₁₆″	...	3,33 cm.
Track Bush diameter ...	...	2″	...	5,08 cm.
Track plate bolt diameter ...	...	⁹⁄₁₆″	...	1,43 cm.
Number of rollers bottom ...	...	8	...	—
Number of rollers top ...	...	2	...	—
Number of plates (each side)... ...	...	30	...	—
Ground contact area ...	1,687 sq. in.	...	10881 cm.2
Pull-bracing grouser area	...	521 sq. in.	...	3360 cm.2
Ground pressure ...	...6.5 lb./sq. in.	...	458 G/cm.2
Operating weight ...	...11,000 lb.	...	4990 Kg.

EXTRA EQUIPMENT

Provision is made for the application of the undernoted ancillary equipment:—

Central Power Take-off
Rear Mounted Belt Pulley (Driven by Power Take-off)
Heavy Duty Haulage Winch
Hydraulic Bulldozer
Hydraulic Angledozer
Driver's Cab
Electric Lighting Equipment
Street Plates
16″ (40,64 cm.) or 18″ (45,92 cm.) Track Plates
Cable Control Unit for use with matched 4/6 cu. yd. Scraper.

SHIPPING SPECIFICATION

Track-Marshall tractor with standard equipment.
Uncased (Protected)
10′ 1″ 307cm. × 5′ 10″ 178cm. × 5″ 4′ 163cm. 96 cwts. 4877 kg.
Top boxed
10′1″ 307cm. × 5′ 10″ 178cm. × 5′4″ 163cm. 99½ cwts. 5055 kg.

In pursuance of this company's policy of constant development, the right is reserved to depart, without notice, from any detail illustrated or specified in this leaflet, without incurring the obligation to provide such modifications on machines previously delivered.

MARSHALL, SONS AND COMPANY LIMITED, GAINSBOROUGH, LINCS., ENGLAND

Telephone: Gainsborough 2301

Telegrams: Marshalls, Gainsborough

Specification for 50 h.p. Track Marshall crawler

Track Marshalls, MP6 and Fowler Challengers on display at the 1957 Royal Smithfield Show London

Track Marshall 50 h.p. crawler with 4-furrow plough circa 1960

Track Marshall 55 fitted with Perkins 270D 4-cylinder engine

physical exertion that was required in steering was hence minimised. The Track Marshall 70 received the identification 70H when equipped with the slewing clutches, whilst the conventional 70 retained the hand-controlled differential steering mechanism and became the 70C.

The 55 also received modifications. A rotary distribution fuel injection pump replaced the previously used in-line pump. Additionally, the fuel combustion was improved and incorporated direct injection. These alterations greatly aided starting and eliminated the tendency of erratic idling.

Throughout the 1960s the Track Marshall continued to increase Marshalls' profit margin. The demand for crawler tractors did not decline on the home market and indeed inclement weather lent itself to increasing demand. Several wet summers in succession had rendered the use of wheeled tractors an impossibility due to water-logged soil. The popularity of the Track Marshall, by the mid 1960s, was such that

Marshalls had gained over 60 per cent of the agricultural market in Britain and were successfully warding off competition from County, International, Fiat and Caterpillar. This improved growth in profits and gave Marshalls the funding to broaden their horizons by venturing into the construction machinery market. In April 1963 Marshalls introduced the first of a series of tracked loading shovels with the release of the Track Marshall 60. The range of operation equipment was also expanded upon, the most significant of which was the hydraulically operated 3-point linkage system. This was the first successful attempt to provide a crawler with the ability to operate mounted farm implements.

In 1964 came a change in colour. Bright yellow was chosen to replace the traditional Fowler orange, partly due to the greater safety awareness of the 1960s. Yellow was more prominent and was different from Fiat, who also finished their crawlers in orange.

The mighty Track Marshall 70 powered by a Perkins 6354 6-cylinder diesel engine

Track Marshall 70 crawler, fitted with cab, attending a steam engine rally in the south-east of England in 1995 (Ross Anderson)

Early Track Marshall 50 h.p. crawler fitted with Perkins L4 diesel engine   (S Gibbard)

Track Marshall 70 fitted with Perkins 6-cylinder 6354 diesel engine

CHAPTER 12

Fading Years

In 1968, Marshall Sons & Company Ltd and John Fowler became part of the Thos Ward group of companies. Ward's control of these two major companies provided the opportunity to unite them as one massive organisation, and in 1970 a new company was formed and traded as Marshall Fowler Ltd.

The initial result of the integration amounted to an updating programme, culminating in the arrival of a much improved and re-styled Track Marshall. The main area to receive change was visually apparent. The rounded appearance of their previous range gave way to a squarer look, with all panelwork manufactured from heavy gauge sheet metal. This provided added protection against damage and corrosion, as well as a much more rugged appearance. The fuel tank was repositioned at the rear of the machine to improve the centre of gravity and prevent spilt fuel from entering the driver's area when refuelling.

Three new versions of the Track Marshall were made available to cater for a wider range of applications. The TM56 replaced the Track Marshall 55, retaining the Perkins 4270D engine that had a slight increase in output to deliver 56 h.p.

The Track Marshall 70 was superseded by the TM75, which continued to employ the Perkins 6354 engine and also had an increase in performance to 75 h.p.

The TM90 was introduced to cater for large scale farming and required additional power to enable it to maintain its ability to haul large implements. The Perkins 6354 engine was again

Track Marshall 56 crawler complete with Marshall angle dozer awaiting collection at Britannia Works, 1988. The late Major Henry Marshall is to the left

An early TM90 with subsoiler

A TM56 in bulldozer form fitted with 28 in low ground pressure track plates

A TM75

A TM90

chosen but was uprated to develop 90 h.p. by increasing the speed from 1700 to 2000 r.p.m.

A new loading shovel was introduced to replace the Track Marshall 60 and 7S. The TM1600, which incorporated the Perkins 6-cylinder engine, had much more power to offer.

In 1970 Bristol Tractors Ltd from Colne, in Lancashire, were acquired by Marshall Fowler. Production of Bristol's range of agricultural tractors was discontinued. However, the Bristol Taurus loading shovel powered by a 3-cylinder Perkins engine was retained and marketed as the TM1100.

The 1970s were a period of turbulence for industry. Britain was affected by the world-wide economic depression, with trade and industry suffering great loss. Inevitably, Marshall Fowler became a victim of the economic decline, and trading throughout the group reflected the impact of the depression as sales figures deteriorated.

As an engineering concern, Marshall Fowler suffered severely. Not only did the Track Marshall division encounter loss but Marshall boilers, wire drawing, tea machinery and the road rollers were all casualties of the set-back in the economy. However, fading sales of the Track Marshall could not solely be blamed upon the economy. The encroachment of 4-wheel drive tractors into areas where crawler tractors had held a dominant presence had to be taken into consideration.

In Britain, a number of companies withdrew from producing crawler tractors to specialise in the 4-wheel drive market. Roadless and County achieved much success with their 4-wheel drive conversions, utilising Ford tractors.

Due to continual trading difficulties, Thos Ward sold their Fowler premises at Hunslet in 1973. Production of the Track Marshall and Fowler Challenger 33 was transferred to Britannia Works. In 1975, Thos Ward sold Marshall Fowler Ltd to British Leyland. Other divisions of the company were also dispersed, including Marshall boilers, wire drawing and tea machinery.

Leyland seized the opportunity to cease production of the Road Marshall roller division, in favour of their own Aveling Barford range. There was much resentment within Marshalls as a result of the decision, due to the superiority of the Road Marshall roller. British Leyland recommenced production of the Track Marshall

range under the control of their industrial division and renamed the new enterprise Aveling Marshall Ltd.

Leyland's funding provided capital for further development. Recognising the increasing growth of large acreage cultivation, Aveling Marshall concentrated upon the high horsepower sector of the crawler market and produced two new additions for their range. The AM100 and AM110 were released in 1975. The AM100 was an uprated version of the TM90 and retained the proven Perkins 6354 engine that had again been uprated to produce 100 h.p. The AM105 defected from Marshalls' committed loyalty to Perkins by offering a 105 h.p. Ford 2715E 6-cylinder engine. Both the AM100 and AM105 were provided with fully enclosed cabs, with optional facility of heating and air-conditioning.

Due to the receding demand for the TM56, production was gradually phased out, which permitted the company to concentrate on their quest to provide crawler tractors with a higher output. Aveling Marshall retained the production of the Fowler Challenger 33 and redistributed it as the AM140. With the exception of increased engine performance, the AM140 had encountered little change since it began life in 1957.

In 1976 the range was furthered by the introduction of the AM120, powered by a Ford 2715E engine. The engine's performance was enhanced somewhat by increasing the engine speed from 1800 to 2200 r.p.m., enabling it to deliver 120 h.p.

Aveling Marshall continued to advance higher in the power struggle and unveiled another addition to their rapidly expanding range. This took place at the 1979 Royal Show, staged at Stoneleigh, in Warwickshire. The AM135 portrayed the progressive advancement in crawler tractor design. Powered by a Perkins turbocharged 6354 6-cylinder engine, the AM135 was capable of delivering 137 h.p. The fully air-conditioned cab provided adequate driver comfort and was equipped with a stereo radio/cassette player as a standard feature.

Before full production of the AM135 commenced, British Leyland announced that they were to divest themselves of their special products group, of which Aveling Marshall were a part. A short period of unrest ensued within the company, whilst their future hung in the balance

The TM135

Assembly line of the Track Marshall 135 crawler, Britannia Works, August 1988

and they faced the grim prospect of closure.

Fortunately, a Lincolnshire farmer and businessman, Charles Nickerson, came to the rescue and purchased Aveling Marshall from Leyland. Nickerson renamed the company Track Marshall Ltd and procured a part of the old establishment at Britannia Works.

The new company continued to manufacture the Aveling Marshall range and focused on flow production of the 135 crawler. A year after its official release, the Track Marshall 135 was finally made available and re-launched at the Royal Show in 1980. The TM135 achieved much success, winning the RASE silver medal in 1981

for its advancement in design.

In an attempt to re-enter the medium power sector of the market, Track Marshall released the 70 h.p. Britannia. The Britannia received a Perkins 4236 4-cylinder engine designed to compete against main competitors Massey Ferguson, Fiat and Universal, which had established a strong presence in Britain with their 70 h.p. crawler tractors.

In 1982 Charles Nickerson purchased the wheeled tractor division from British Leyland and re-registered the company as Marshall Sons & Company Ltd, with Track Marshall Ltd becoming a holding company. Leylands' tractor

Track Marshall re-entered their medium power sector of the market with their 70 h.p. Britannia in August 1983

The late Major Henry Marshall with a consignment of Leyland and Marshall wheeled tractors at Britannia Works
(D Sidwells)

Leyland 702 tractor badged as the Marshall 702 after the Nickerson take-over in 1982

manufacturing facilities were transferred from their Bathgate factory in Scotland to Gainsborough, where production recommenced under the Marshall banner.

Fundamentally, the wheeled tractors manufactured at Britannia Works were a continuation of Leylands' wide range and had encountered little change, except for a certain amount of badge engineering. The range catered for a wide variation in horsepower, tractors being available in sizes from 30 to 92 h.p.

In 1984 the Field Marshall name was resurrected in Marshalls' first full venture back into production of wheeled tractors since the demise of the MP6 in 1961. The Field Marshall 100 and 115 were born and bred at Britannia Works to fulfil the demand for higher output. The Marshall 100 received a 103 h.p. Leyland 698 engine. With the provision of a turbocharger, the 698 developed 116 h.p. and was installed into the Marshall 115. The introduction of the new models enabled Marshalls to boast a comprehensive range of tractors consisting of 23 different models, a majority of which offered the provision of 4-wheel drive.

Despite Charles Nickerson's ambitious attempts to establish a position in the wheeled tractor market, strong competition from tractor giants Ford, Massey Ferguson, John Deere and Case prevented any area of growth. With the exception of the Marshall 100 and 115 tractors, the Marshall tractor range had not advanced sufficiently and was fundamentally derivative of the former Nuffield tractor that had long been outdated.

Shortly after the Track Marshall 135's release, it encountered a number of teething troubles with the final drive assembly. Many of these tractors were returned to the factory where they underwent an extensive modification programme, substantially reducing any profit.

It became increasingly evident that all was not well within the company, which was faced with a minimal number of orders for the wheeled tractors, plus the high costs involved in developing new tractors. As a result of heavy losses amounting

Gainsborough born and bred Marshall 100 tractor, introduced in 1984

to £12.5 million, Marshalls were once again called into receivership.

Herbert Flatters, a former director of Marshalls, was reluctant to see the Track Marshall crawler division slip into history while retaining future potential. In January 1986, Flatters acquired Track Marshall from the receivers and renamed the new company Track Marshall of Gainsborough Ltd. The wheeled division was sold separately to the Bentall Simplex company. Bentall Simplex transferred production of the Marshall wheeled tractors to their premises at Scunthorpe and retained the Marshall name, trading as Marshall Tractors Ltd. Unfortunately the Marshall wheeled tractor continued to remain

unpopular, despite the introduction of new models that featured the popular Perkins built engines, and production of the range was eventually phased out. Bentall Simplex were not willing to give up on their venture into the tractor industry. In 1989 they negotiated with Steyr-Daimler-Puch from Austria and distributed the Steyr range of tractors in Britain, under the Marshall banner. In 1989 Bentall Simplex renamed the tractor company Marshall Daimler Ltd and provided a new range of 2-wheel and 4-wheel drive tractors, ranging from 62 to 150 h.p. This agreement was terminated in 1991 when Steyr opened their own British franchise distribution network.

Marshall badged 5744 Steyr tractor

Turbo charged Marshall 125 introduced in 1986 under the control of Marshall Tractors (Scunthorpe) Ltd

As a gesture to regain customer confidence because of the difficulties with the TM135, Herbert Flatters conducted a modification programme. This enabled customers to return their machines to Britannia Works where the necessary repairs were undertaken, tractors within the warranty period being repaired free of charge. Others were chargeable but at a special reduced rate, with Track Marshall absorbing a large proportion of the costs.

The inclement weather during the summers of 1983 and 1984 again led to a demand for crawler tractors, which resulted in a steady flow of orders for the Track Marshall and in particular the TM135. Due to the popularity of the TM135 and the request for higher output, Track Marshall headed further up the horsepower scale and introduced the TM155. It received the proven Perkins 6354.4 turbocharged engine, provided in the TM135. However, the engine speed had been

The improved rubber tracked TM200 crawler
(J Blackbeard)

somewhat increased, from 2200 to 2500 r.p.m., which enabled it to deliver the required 155 h.p.

The sudden death of Herbert Flatters in 1987, at the age of 56, resulted in the formation of a new Board of Directors, consisting of Flatters' wife Eileen and his son Glenn. Due to economic depression and rising interest rates, the Flatters family found the trend of business extremely difficult. The increasing pressure of rival manufacturers' crawler tractors, at home and abroad, had blighted sales and led to a rapid decline in orders. Once again the outlook was bleak for the Track Marshall crawler, as the Flatters family encountered ensuing financial difficulties. Tom Walkinshaw, a good friend and associate of the Flatters family, had expressed an interest in Track Marshall for many years. He maintained control of his own enterprising business, the Tom Walkinshaw Racing (TWR) group, and owned the neighbouring Compak packaging company, that had been established by Charles Nickerson in 1983. Tom Walkinshaw was a renowned genius in the world of mechanical engineering and was also well known throughout the motor racing fraternity for his formation of

the TWR Jaguar racing team. After a series of negotiations, the TWR group announced in May 1990 that through their industrial division they had purchased Track Marshall of Gainsborough from the Flatters family.

The name Track Marshall of Gainsborough was retained, under the control of the TWR group, and production continued at Britannia Works. New funds permitted the continuation of current models, although as a result of pursuing the higher power sector of the market, production of the 70 h.p. Britannia was gradually phased out.

Development of a new revolutionary crawler tractor was underway in 1989, emulating the Caterpillar rubber track principle. The Track Marshall 200 was powered by a 200 h.p. Cummins engine and made its first public debut at the 1990 Royal Show. The provision of rubber tracks enabled it to travel on the road without damaging the surface, thus eliminating the major disadvantage of the crawler tractor. The tractor offered the benefits of crawler tractor adhesion and low ground pressure, whilst providing speed, manoeuvrability and the comfort of a wheeled tractor. Priced at £95,000 the TM200 was perhaps

A 155 h.p. TM155 crawler, still available on a made to order basis

a little out of reach for the majority of British farmers, who were suffering as a result of the economic depression. Problems arose among the few that were sold, as customers experienced failures with the Australian manufactured tracks which led to a number of costly warranty claims.

Despite the incorporation of a number of improvements comprising an increase in output to 210 h.p., enhanced visibility and Goodyear rubber tracks, the demand for the TM200 remained disappointing. The continued recession, coupled with several dry seasons and the increasing popularity of 4-wheel drive tractors, amounted to a further fall in orders, and production of the TM200 was gradually phased out.

Inevitably the deterioration in orders worsened and production of their conventional crawlers was reduced considerably. By 1994, a decision was made to manufacture machines on a built-to-order basis. Production lines and machining tools were dispersed of, necessitating outside contract for any further manufacturing.

As we go to press, Track Marshall of Gainsborough remains with us but in a much smaller capacity. The company occupy a small part of the old Britannia Works premises, where they undertake repairs and servicing of customers' machines and continue to manufacture the TM155 crawler tractor on a strictly made-to-order basis.

Bibliography and Further Reading

BOOKS

British Tractors for World Farming
Michael Williams,
Blandford Press, Poole, Dorset.

Farm Machinery
Claude Culpin,
Crosby Lockwood & Son Ltd, London.

Great Tractors
Michael Williams,
Blandford Press, Poole, Dorset.

Know Your Tractor
Shell Petroleum Co. Ltd.

Machinery on the Farm
Thomas Huthinson,
Blackie & Son Ltd, London.

The Marshall-Fowler Album
(pictorial history of Marshall and Fowler tractors)
Allan T Condie,
A T Condie Publications.

Sixty Famous Tractors
Allan T Condie,
A T Condie Publications.

Sixty Tractors of World War Two
Allan T Condie,
A T Condie Publications.

The Story of the Britannia Iron Works
(history of Marshall Sons & Co)
Michael Lane,
Quiller Press, London.

The Story of the Steam Plough Works
(history of John Fowler & Co.(Leeds) Ltd)
Michael Lane,
Northgate Publishing Co. Ltd, London.

Tractors on the Farm
H J Hine,
Farmer & Stockbreeder, London.

PERIODICALS/NEWSPAPERS

Engineering

The Engineering

Farm Implement and Machinery Review

Farm Mechanization

Farmer & Stockbreeder

Farmers Weekly

Marshall publications:
Britannia News,
quarterly newsletter of the Field Marshall
Tractors Club, edited by Peter Anderson

Marshall Group

Marshall Mettle

Power Farmer

Power Farming

Conversion Table

LENGTH

1 in (inch)	25.4 mm
1 ft (foot)	300 mm
12 in (1 ft)	0.30 m
3 ft (1 yard)	0.91m

PRESSURE

p.s.i.	pounds per square inch
CFM	cubic feet per minute

VOLUME

8 pints	1 gallon
1 gallon	4.6 litres

MONEY

£ s d	pounds, shillings, pence
£1	20 shillings
1 shilling	12 pence
240 pence	100 new pence (£)

WEIGHT

1 lb (pound)	0.45 kg
112 lb	1 hundredweight (cwt)
1 hundredweight	50.8 kg
20 hundredweight	1 ton
1 ton	1016 kg

POWER

1 horsepower	0.746 kilowatt
1 kilowatt	1.34 horsepower

Index

FARMING PRESS

Below is a sample of the wide range of agricultural and veterinary books and videos we publish. For more information or for a free illustrated catalogue of all our publications please contact:

Farming Press
Miller Freeman plc
2 Wharfedale Road, Ipswich IP1 4LG, United Kingdom
Telephone (01473) 241122 Fax (01473) 240501

Massey on Parade (VIDEO)

**FARMING PRESS WITH THE
ONTARIO AGRICULTURAL MUSEUM**

Covers key points and major developments in Massey-Harris's machinery output, focusing mainly on tractors, but including other equipment. Features the recollections of Massey-Harris users interviewed during the 150th anniversary celebration of the Massey company in Ontario, Canada.

The Massey Legacy Volume One

JOHN FARNWORTH

A highly illustrated and comprehensive review of the vast range of products manufactured by Massey Ferguson and its predecessor companies over the last 150 years. In this first volume information is included on agricultural tractors, key people in company development, chronology, company and product promotion, cultivation equipment and planting equipment. Price lists and sales data are also given.

Change on the Land

STUART GIBBARD

A collection of outstanding photographs which illustrate the revolution in farming techniques that has taken place over the past 100 years. The reader is taken on a journey from the days when horses reigned supreme, through steam power, to the present age of high spec tractors.

County Tractors (VIDEO)

STUART GIBBARD

From trucks and crawlers to the 188 hp, 1884 tractor - the story of County's Ford-based conversions is followed through archive film extracts.

Stationary Engine Review

PATRICK KNIGHT

The cream of stationary engine manufacturers and models selected to give a clear insight into the wide range of engines produced during their heyday. Authoritative text and a superb collection of pictures.

Ford and Fordson Tractors
Massey Ferguson Tractors

MICHAEL WILLIAMS

Two heavily illustrated guides to the models which made these leading companies great.

Farming Press is a division of Miller Freeman plc which provides a wide range of media services in agriculture and allied businesses. Among the magazines published by the group are *Arable Farming, Dairy Farmer, Farming News* and *Pig Farming*. For a specimen copy of any of these please contact the address above.